DRIVE FOR SHOW, PUTT FOR DOUGH

Nine Holes of Golf with God

Andrew R. Linch

urbanpress

Drive for Show, Putt for Dough
by Andrew R. Linch
Copyright © 2019 Andrew R. Linch

ISBN # 978-1-63360-106-2

For Worldwide Distribution Printed in the U.S.A.

Urban Press
P.O. Box 8881
Pittsburgh, PA 15221-0881 USA
412.646.2780
www.urbanpress.us

PART ONE

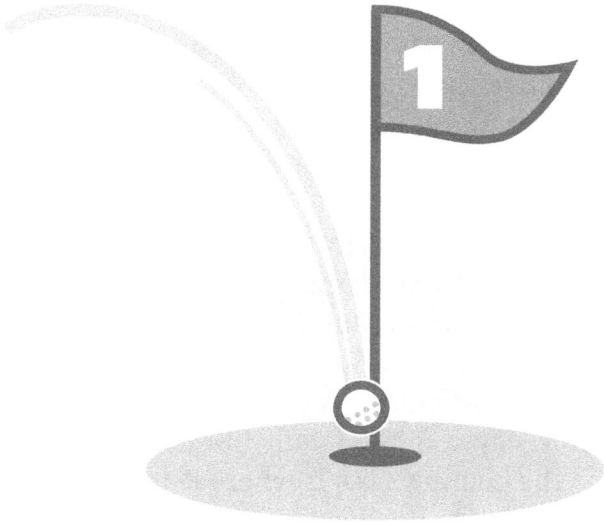

The Tournament

It was the week of the state championship. Peter Young's father, Robert Young, reminded him that no 18-year-old had ever won a state golf championship before, and he would be going up against some awesome, experienced players. That said, Robert told him, "I believe in you, Son, and anything is possible with God. I'm praying for you to play your best."

Peter listened politely to his Dad, but inwardly thought, *Yes, it's never happened, but there's never been an 18-year-old like me, and I* **will** *win, with or without God's help.*

In Peter's mind, the tournament was going to come down to two golfers and they could not have provided a greater contrast. There was Peter, whose father was a member of the municipal golf club and thus Peter was a member too. Peter didn't like what the club represented. He wanted to move up and on from the municipal course. The tournament was to be at the country club course, the other course in town, and Peter had managed to sneak in some practice as he went moonlight walking on the course and played the holes. On the day of the qualifying round, he found it quite easy and qualified second behind Bud, who shot a 65 to Peter's 66. They were seven and six under par respectively.

Bud was Peter's main rival, and the reigning state champion. Bud's father was a member at the country club as was Bud. He came from old money and it showed. He was cocky and arrogant, feeling he "belonged" at the club. He radiated entitlement, an attitude nurtured by his parents. The locals all said the money stayed in the family but the class had left a generation ago. The country club is where Peter wanted to be and he was determined to get there, and it started in his mind by winning the tournament and defeating Bud.

Peter wanted to win the championship for many reasons, one being the loss of his mother the year prior. His feeling of loss remained, but he and his dad never spoke about it. Winning was his way out of feeling the loss—or so he thought. He simply had to win for winning was becoming a way of life for him.

The first day of the championship saw Peter and Bud distance themselves from the rest of the pack. They both shot a 66, and the rest were at least six to ten shots behind them. Peter did it the traditional way by consistently hitting the fairway and greens. The course had five par-five holes, which were birdie material if played correctly. Peter was long off the tee and did exactly that. He also picked up another two birdies along the way. Bud was also long though a little wayward, but his recovery skills from the rough were good so it didn't cost him.

Day two was a slightly windy day but even though the scoring average for the championship was three shots higher, both Bud and Peter shot a 67. At the end of the day, it was a two-horse race and everyone knew it. The local paper termed it David versus Goliath, which Peter and his dad found amusing. His dad joked, "I don't think they have you down as Goliath, which is good because we know the outcome of that one." While Peter usually resented the Bible references, the thought of him being David defeating Goliath gave him great pleasure.

On day three, or moving day as it's called on tour, both players put the pedal down and tried to make it count. Both Peter and Bud moved even farther away from the rest of the field with aggressive but accurate play, with Bud shooting a 64 and Peter besting him by one with the best score of the week at 63. While playing the last par hole on the back nine, both players hit over the dogleg, which enabled them to reach the green. Bud had slightly pulled his drive into the rough. Up to this point, Bud's recovery skills were something with which even Peter was impressed, so he watched with interest as Bud and his caddie, Slick, who worked for Bud's dad, walked up to their ball.

From Peter's view, the ball was behind a clump of tall, wild grass. Bud would have to wedge that back to the fairway, giving him a long third shot to the green. Peter knew this because he had been in a similar position one evening on one of his practice drives. *Good luck,* thought Peter, *not even Superman could get it to the green from there.*

Bud walked up the fairway to survey the green with all eyes on him, but for some reason Peter glanced back at Slick to see his leg twist like he was side footing something. Peter's mind was spinning: *Did I really see what I just saw?* When Bud came back, his ball stood two feet to the right and clear of the large tuft of wild grass, a much better lie. From there, Bud easily got the ball to the green. Peter pulled himself together and finished the round with a twenty-foot putt for birdie to take a one-shot lead into the last round. As they shook hands at the end, Slick barely made eye contact with

Peter, who was trying to stay focused, but everything in him wanted to scream, "You two cheated!"

That night, Peter wrestled with whether he should talk to his dad or someone about the cheating. After mulling it over for two hours, he fell into a deep sleep, concluding that he was the better golfer and would beat Bud anyway, whether he cheated or not.

In the morning, Peter and his dad kept the breakfast talk light, but before they left the table, his dad looked at Peter and said, "Win or lose, Son, I am so proud of you. I just want you to know that."

"Thanks, Dad," said Peter, who looked down at his golf shoes and then added, "Hey, but while we're here, we might as well win it, right?" Robert nodded his agreement and they hugged, both desperately wanting the win for differing reasons connected to their loss—Peter, who needed something positive to think about, and Robert, for his son's well-being.

At the first tee, Bud had a calm and assured look like he owned the course, which was not surprising given that he seldom heard the word no or tasted defeat—thanks to his talent coupled with his dad's money. In Bud's mind, it was inevitable that he would win, so being one shot behind was simply an inconvenience, not worthy of being called a problem.

Peter, on the other hand, found himself nervous for the first time in the tournament. He soon recovered when his dad squeezed his shoulder and whispered, "You got this, Son." With his calm restored, the round commenced.

Both players were aggressive in all aspects of their game and the three-hundred-plus crowd knew they were in for a display of fine golf, and were not disappointed. On the third hole, Bud holed a thirty-five-foot putt for birdie to draw even with Peter. With the rest of the field not mounting any attack, it was down to these two gladiators to fight it out in a bloodless but no less savage display of winner-take-all.

On the fourth hole, a par five, Peter rammed in a twenty-foot eagle putt to beat Bud's tap-in birdie to go one up again. Walking to the next hole, Peter turned to his father, "It's time to put the hammer down, Dad, and push in all the chips." Peter had an intensity on his face that even surprised his father. From then on, it was like a match when both fighters give and take punches without flinching.

By the end of the front nine, both players were five under par and Peter held onto his slender one-stroke lead. Unbelievably, from the tenth hole on, both players raised the ante even more, neither giving an inch and both pushing the boundaries of their ability.

At the fourteenth hole it happened, another chink in Bud's armour. Both players had birdied two of the last three holes, but at the fourteenth hole, Bud made a mistake on his tee shot. This hole was a long par four and despite the distance, a player still needed to hit the fairway to be sure of a par. A shot from the rough would prevent a golfer from getting the necessary spin to stay on the green, and his ball would end up trickling ever so slowly but purposefully into the valley running around the entire green. Worse still, there were no bunkers on this hole. The greenkeeper always let the grass in the valley grow to three inches in length, causing a player to pitch out with little spin so if the pitch was not on point, the player would simply see the ball come trundling back to his feet.

Peter felt this was his chance to move ahead so he could relax, at least a little, over the remaining holes and enjoy a triumphant walk up to eighteen alongside his dad. Then it happened again. He was on the fairway twenty yards ahead of Bud when he noticed that Bud's ball had moved again, with his caddie Slick close by.

Peter walked back to Bud's ball only to have a rules official intercept him. "Young man, what's the problem?" When Peter indicated he only wanted to check out Bud's lie, the official told him to go back to his own ball and not cause a scene. It was then that Peter made his accusation: "That ball was moved."

At that moment, Bud returned to his ball, but Slick vehemently denied it and Bud defended his caddie's integrity. Peter's father now stood at his shoulder, so close he could feel the support radiating from him. Peter then noticed the identical rings on the official's and Bud's fingers and it clicked. *They are Masons*, thought Peter. He knew that bond was unbreakable and that this confrontation was going nowhere.

"I must have been mistaken," Peter said, looking Bud straight in the eye, and to his annoyance Bud appeared to smirk at him. Slick, his caddie, suddenly found something interesting on the ground to look at rather than look Peter in the eye. Peter turned and started walking back to his ball.

As Peter went back to his ball, Peter's dad said, "You know he moved the ball and I know it too." Robert was angry, and said, "It's not fair. It's not right. I'm going to protest."

"No, you're not, Dad, it's over. Did you see their rings? Their part of the local Masonic lodge. They'll stick together," Peter explained.

That made Robert even more angry, and he practically spat out his next words, "I'm going to pray that God will help you, Peter," but Peter stopped listening and thought, *I don't need your prayers or anyone's prayers. Those prayers didn't save my mom and they won't help me. I'm going to beat Bud straight up.*

Back at his ball, Peter turned to watch Bud, who settled over his ball and hit his best shot of the day, landing fifteen feet short of the hole and rolling to within two feet. Peter felt like he had been punched in the stomach, but had to face the fact he needed to release the anger. Only then could he play a controlled shot, which he needed to do now more than at any other time in the tournament.

Peter played his shot but the moment he hit it, he realized it was hit with anger that was still coursing through him. As such, it flew ten yards farther and did not match Bud's. His ball came to rest in the three-inch collar surrounding the green, the very place Peter had not wanted to be. There was silence for a moment from Peter and his father. A moment ago, he felt like he was going to get a cushion and stride up 18 victorious like Caesar entering Rome after a victory. Now he was looking at a possible two-shot swing in Bud's direction. "Okay, Son, let's find that ball and chip it in."

They descended the slope to Peter's ball, which was half way down the three-inch grass but not at the bottom of the grass. The bottom would have been preferable, for the ball's position made a difficult shot even harder. Pete realized that the bump-and-run shot had been taken out of the equation because if he tried it and failed it, would just land weakly halfway up the slope and come back to his feet. His only option was to open up his 56-degree sand wedge. The risk factor on this shot was off the chart and the only thing going for him was that there was no other option.

Peter descended the slope and took one last look and settled over the ball. It seemed as if from nowhere but at that moment he saw and heard the voice of the Scottish pro: "Wee man, if you can believe it, even if you have trouble seeing it, all things are possible." Peter actually smiled and settled over the ball, weight on his rear foot, club face 10 degrees open, and with one last breath, he swung. The contact was perfect and the ball rose with enough forward momentum and height. The shot was almost everything Peter had wished for as it went up and started to descend.

Peter ran up the slope in a vain hope that somehow his close proximity to the ball would help it to achieve the impossible. The ball landed two inches from the hole and stopped in its own shadow. The applause from the crowd was deafening for they realized the skill and audacity of the shot. Bud lined up his putt and stroked the ball, but before it was halfway there, Peter knew it was in. They were now even after fourteen holes.

The fifteenth hole was uneventful in that both men did what they had to do to save par. The sixteenth was the last par five on the back nine. Both wanted to stamp their authority on this hole, which at 490 yards was in reach for both of them. The hole was a slight dogleg right protected by bunkers. All they needed to do was stay clear of the bunkers.

Peter's shot went past Bud's by 30 yards, leaving him only a 160 yards to the not-so-distant flag. Robert said, "Stay calm and focused," but somewhere in the back of his mind, Robert felt something was wrong, but he shook it off. They both stood towards one side as Bud played his shot from 190 yards out. His swing looked good to Peter, and the applause from the green said it was very close. It was then that Peter and his father realized they had been played because of the rules in classic match play.

Peter's father remembered that Bud had gripped down on his driver to take a little distance off to allow him to play first. It was a bold move but in match play, which is what this had turned into, the strategy is to apply pressure to your opponent by playing your second shot first and getting it close.

Peter realized he had been played by Bud and he had to gather his wits about him or he was in trouble. Peter took a moment and closed his eyes, trying to gather himself. After visualising the shot with his eight iron, Peter settled over the ball and swung. To the spectators, the shot appeared fine but the ball came to rest ten yards short of Peter's normal shot. Peter grimaced as he knew that he was trying to regain control of his game but it felt like he was fighting the law of gravity itself.

Peter asked his dad for the same eight iron he had used

on his previous shot. His dad handed the club over but knew this was a mistake. He knew Peter was looking for redemption for his previous mistake but there was none to be had. He wanted to tell his son that but it seemed the wrong time to do so. Both Peter and his dad were battling inner turmoil though in different ways.

Peter settled over the ball but not before glancing at Bud to see him smiling at his caddie and winking. Peter swung the eight iron and made perfect contact, but before the chipped ball had even landed, both Peter and his father knew the ball would have to hit the flagstick to avoid going past it and into the ridge. The ball rolled towards the hole at a pace that suggested it was being drawn there by a magnet. Hope started to rise in both player and caddie, but then the ball hit the slightest of imperfections and swerved to the right.

The ball carried on like a lemming determined to throw itself into the sea. The ball hit the small ridge and ended up 15 feet from the hole. Peter felt the wind knocked out of his sails for he had gone all in and lost. He rallied himself and made a valiant effort to putt for birdie but it ran past six inches on the low side, leaving him a simple tap in for par, which after his heroics off the tee felt like a bogey.

Peter stood to one side in a daze. He knew all he was waiting for now was to see Bud bury his eagle putt. Bud was strutting around the green like a proud peacock lining up his putt. It was small consolation that Bud actually missed his simple putt, but tapped in for a birdie and a one-shot lead.

Peter walked to seventeen feeling like it was over—and it was. Bud had cheated, but he was way experienced a golfer to relinquish his lead. Peter succumbed to the mental anguish and shot one over par over the last two holes, while Bud held par for a two-stroke victory and the state championship.

Bud was all smiles at the trophy dinner and presentation. He spoke well of his courageous playing partner and how Peter, six years his junior, had a bright future ahead of him in golf. He said he will surely be state champion one year soon. Peter heard the words and tried to smile but he could no more swallow them than he could swallow his dinner, which remained on his plate.

That night, Peter decided it wasn't worth it to play or live by the rules. He was angry—at his father for all his religious platitudes and attempts to console him that his loss was God's will and would be an opportunity for growth. He was angry that God had not helped him, even though he was the one who played fairly. In the days ahead, Peter made some decisions that would guide his life for years to come. Golf and life were all about winning and from then on, he would do whatever it took to be victorious, like Bud had done in that state championship.

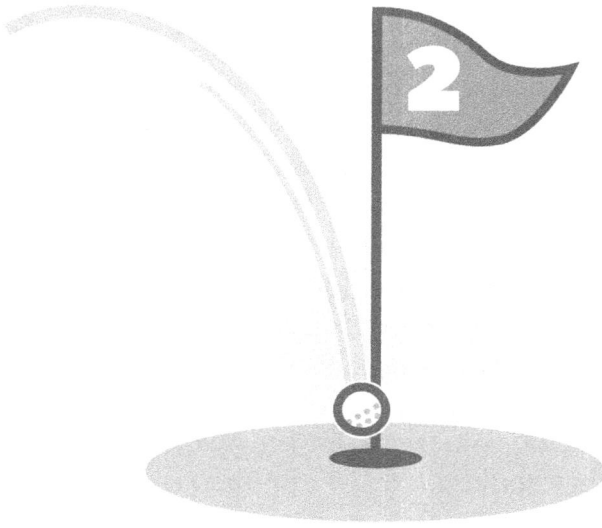

The Guest Player

Many years later, Peter eased his new BMW M3 out of his personal parking spot that read "Peter Davis, Vice President of Sales", a title he loved. He had fought tooth and nail to get it, bled for it, and still had plans to go higher. He had once shared his business philosophy with his wife and it was simple: "I want all my toys and everybody else's toys as well."

Peter worked for Drexochem, the third largest pharmaceutical company in the world. Their company motto was "to heal and cure the world's diseases." In the sales department, however, the motto was a little different: "We will not rest until the whole world is using our drugs." Peter often dreamt of what his bonus would be if they could get seven billion people using Drexochem drugs. That thought would always make him smile and exhale slowly as he added up the zeros. His wife had once asked what the difference was between him and a drug dealer. He laughingly replied, "The government helps me sell drugs but arrests the dealer."

Once in the car, Peter gunned it out of the parking lot, listening appreciatively to the 444 hp V6 roar through the custom M3 exhaust as some would listen to and enjoy classical music. It was a beautiful Friday afternoon and life was truly good. Peter's sales team had worked hard to achieve their monthly targets and earn their bonuses. They had overpromised on what they could deliver and some of the drugs were controversial, but that didn't concern Peter or his team. He wanted to win all the business he could and that meant doing whatever it took to make the sale. They would deal with the fallout when they could not deliver on their sales promises.

Speaking of winning, Peter was off to the Drexochem Country Club to play golf. (Drexochem had bought a major share in the club at Peter's recommendation.) Since it had a higher-than-normal percentage of doctors as members, golf was not a hobby for Peter; it was an obsession. His wife described it as "the other woman in their marriage." As much as he tried to get her to play, she flat out refused, reasoning that one golf-obsessed person in the house was enough.

Peter was the reigning club champion for two years running, but of course, that was not enough for him. This year's tournament was two weeks away and he was desperate to win, which would make him the first person in the club's history to achieve a "three-peat" as members were referring to it at the club. The win would make him the "Big Dog" and would hopefully lead to becoming Club Captain—another title he coveted. In his case, it wasn't only the title but also how the title would open doors and help him network and schmooze with company execs on the work front. That would be a double win, and Peter was all about winning, not just some things but everything.

Peter had it all planned out. His handicap was plus four, best in the club. He was playing well, and knew he was head-and-shoulders above the next best player in the club because he had played him often enough. He had even beaten Brad, the club pro, for the first time the previous week. This was another notch on his belt because the pro had been a PGA tour player for four seasons, only to stop when his wife gave birth to their first child, a girl with a congenital heart problem. From what Peter heard, her care took all the money they had. To Peter, Brad seemed like a broken man. He'd gone from the tour to an ordinary life and seemed grateful for the regular paycheck the club provided. While Peter understood Brad's reasons for leaving the tour, deep down he considered him a loser.

Peter's goal today was off to get in a quick nine holes, playing from the championship tees of course. He knew he needed to practice from those tees to set him up for the upcoming tournament. After Peter eased the M3 into the club's parking lot, he confidently strode towards the clubhouse and changing rooms. Just as he was about to go in, Brad called out to him, "Peter, can you do me a huge favor?" Brad did not wait for a response because Peter was not in the habit of doing favors unless there was something in it for him. Brad continued, "I've got a really good player and I just gave him a lesson. He wants to play the course but since he's never played here before, he thought it would be good for him to have a partner. Would you play with him?"

There was more silence from Peter, and Brad added, "You never know. He could teach you a thing or two," appealing to Peter's pride that told him few people had anything to teach him. "Oh and Peter, I think this guys a high roller. He had some serious money in his wallet. Said he's a cash-only kind of guy. I know how you like a gamble, so you can probably win a few bucks." Brad was pushing all Peter's buttons and knew money was the biggest one. The last one got the response Brad was hoping for.

"Okay, Brad, what the heck." *A little fresh meat for the*

champ to chew up will make for a fun afternoon, he thought. "I would love to play your guy. Hope you warned him that he's about to become a sacrificial lamb."

Brad smiled and shook his head. "He'll find out in due time. Thanks! I'll go tell him to be on the first tee in 15 minutes. His name's Ben, by the way, CEO of some international company, I think. You're kind of guy." Deep down, Brad was thinking, *I hope this guy Ben is as good as I think he is. It would be so good to see Peter get thrashed for a change.*

Peter went into the clubhouse to change. As he did, he thought about what Brad had said that Ben was "my kind of guy." Peter had come a long way from being the son of a small-town plumber and provided quite a contrast to his father, a plumber who worked hard, valued God, and always put his family first—but didn't have much to show for it. He had constantly talked about God's purpose for Peter's life, much to Peter's annoyance.

On the other hand, Peter loved his wife but they both knew the sacrifices needed to have the lifestyle they were enjoying, so business success was first and foremost—which meant lots of company-sponsored evening dinners, golf outings, and travel. There was no time for church, for Sundays were often golf days and time to rest from a hectic weekday schedule.

Despite Peter's approach to life, his dad had quietly resolved not to give up on his son coming back to church and to his senses, for Robert saw Peter become more and more consumed with work, success, and things—and told him so on several occasions. This annoyed Peter, for he saw it as his dad being "religious." The only interest they seemed to share any more was golf, and they loved to play the local municipal golf course, although it was getting more and more difficult for Peter to find the time.

Truth be told, his dad was a good player who, on

more than one occasion, had scores well below the par for the course. Peter smiled as he remembered one of those below-par rounds during one of their regular friendly Saturday morning games when he was a boy. His dad had broken the course record with a 62 on the tricky par 71 layout and was quite underwhelmed about it. Peter would have been bragging and showing off, but not his dad. His only comment was "It was a good game, Son."

Peter felt he was way beyond the municipal course, even though it held fond memories of growing up and the summer when the visiting Scottish pro had profoundly impacted Peter and his dad. Right now, Peter had more important things to think about, like the visitor who was about to get a lesson in how to play the Drexochem course.

Peter approached the first tee and gave Ben the once over. *Average*, he thought, *average height, average build, in fact everything about him is average, even his clothes.* There were no logos on his clothing, even though his clothing looked very good quality. Peter remembered his dad again, because quality and not branding were not his things to emphasize. In sharp contrast, Peter was six feet one inches tall, wore Hugo Boss golf attire, and had been told he was pretty good looking by the ladies on his sales team.

"Hello," said Peter.

"Hello there" replied Ben.

Peter at once noticed Ben's eyes. He couldn't find the word to describe them. For a moment, Ben's gaze made him feel out of kilter. Then it came to him. *Ben's eyes are deep, like the eyes of someone who has seen it all—and I feel like I have met him someplace before.* Yet instead of being cynical, Ben's friendly attitude suggested he still cared after all he had been through and seen. *Wow*, thought Peter, *he would make a great salesman.*

Ben put his hand out. "Nice to meet you, Peter. I've

heard good things about you from Brad," he added with a wink. "I'm in town for a while and love the game. Brad gave me a lesson and then was kind enough to lend me his clubs. I used to play a bit but work got in the way. As a CEO of a company that operates worldwide, I don't feel good taking the afternoon off to play golf while my team is hard at it."

Peter wasn't phased. His introductory remarks simply confirmed to Peter that Ben was a loser. *If you're the CEO, you can take all the time you want and need. You're the boss.*

"Anyway," Ben continued, "I used to be pretty good, but I'm a bit rusty now."

"You said Brad lent you his clubs? Nice of him," replied Peter. Peter knew that Brad, like most good golfers, did not like others playing with his clubs. Peter thought, *He must be going soft.*

"What's your handicap" Ben?" Peter inquired.

"Plus four," said Ben.

"Same as me," said Peter, trying not to sound surprised at the realisation that they were the same handicap. "Okay, so we can play off scratch. In fact, why don't we have a little side bet on the game, say $100 dollars a hole, or is that a bit steep for you?" Peter was in full alpha-male, competitive mode.

"Fine, but if you'd prefer, I can go a $1,000 a hole," Ben suggested.

What the hell? thought Peter. Maintaining his poker face, he asked himself, *Is this guy hustling me or just trying to get into my head?* "Heck, why not? My wife could do with some new outfits," said Peter, smiling his nicest smile. At that, the men shook hands again and the game was on.

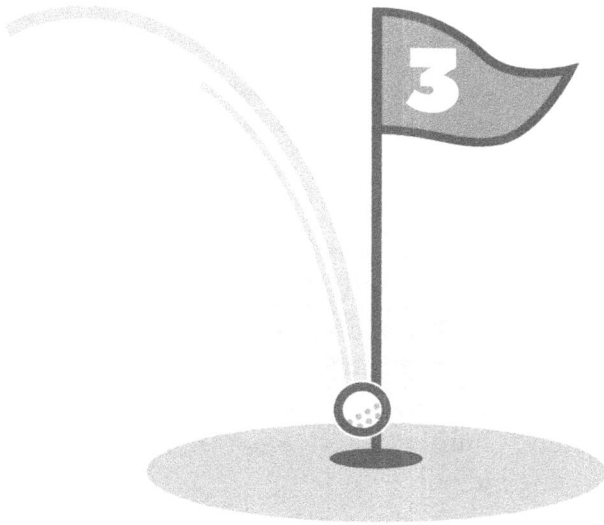

Game On

Peter thought, *You're mine! You're rusty, don't know the course, and you're using someone else's clubs. This will be over before it's even started.* He made a magnanimous gesture towards the first tee and said, "Guests first."

Ben smiled, "Thanks partner, but really, I would like you to show me the way. I mean you are the big dog here," he said and sounded like he meant it, "so please, *you* go first."

Peter took his driver out and moved toward the tee. As he did, he described the hole to Ben. *Because I'm going to gut him like a fish doesn't mean I can't be civil.* "This hole is 440 yards from the championship tees, which is where we're playing from. It's a dogleg right at 200 yards off the tee," Peter explained.

"Thanks. Actually, this reminds me of a course I once played in St. John's," Ben commented. The comment took Peter back. "St John's?" he asked and Ben confirmed what Peter had heard him say. Peter didn't say anything, but he didn't think *anyone* knew where St. John's was. It was not known for anything great and he certainly wasn't about to let on to Ben that he had grown up there.

St. John's was a typical small American town back when Peter was growing up. Despite having a population of only 12,000, there were two golf courses there. One was a municipal course, typically attended by locals who couldn't afford the big fees at the private country club. Peter grew up on the municipal golf course. Now that he thought about it, the first hole at Drexochem Country Club was not unlike the ninth hole at St. John's Municipal.

When Peter described the hole to Ben, he conveniently left out that being a dogleg right at 200 yards off the tee, the golfer had to fade the ball around the corner to be able to play to the green in two shots. If the golfer's fade turned into a slice, it was the trees for him—not a nice way to start a round.

Peter put his new Titleist Pro V1 ball on the tee and placed his grip on his custom-made driver. He positioned himself to his line, took one last look at his target, which was left-hand side of the fairway, and swung the club. As soon as he made contact with the ball, he could hear it was perfect. It had the fade spin he intended and the ball landed about 285 yards from the tee and rolled out—in total, a 305-yard drive, perfectly positioned on the right side of the fairway. This left him the best angle to the pin, about 135 yards away. "Great drive," Ben said with a chuckle. "I'll be happy to be anywhere near that shot."

"Oh yes, you would," said Peter with a laugh and as much charm as he could manage, trying not to be smug about it.

Ben removed the cover from his driver and stepped up. He placed his ball on the tee peg, looked down the fairway, and beamed. Peter saw this and wondered what he was smiling about. *Ha*, he thought, *he won't be smiling for long.* He studied Ben, wanting to learn his weaknesses and strengths, just like he did as a salesman.

As Peter studied Ben, he had a sense that he was looking at his father, which was strange because Ben looked nothing like him. His father was taller with a different complexion and hair color. Peter could see no faults in Ben's setup and grip as he expected, given he was a plus-four handicap. Ben started his back swing, and as he did, Peter had to hold in a gasp. Everything Ben did worked together. It was effortless, elegant, and powerful, all in one move.

Ben's swing was perfect and that didn't adequately describe it. Peter struggled for the right words. All he could think was it was like watching a child swing a golf club but with the strength of a big cat and with the golf knowledge only great players like Hogan, Nicklaus, or Tiger possessed. The sound at impact was incredible, what one only ever hears when a top golfer strikes the ball.

Ben's ball took off on a similar line to Peter's. It was low and hissing, full of energy as it slowly rose to its apex and descended until it hit the fairway, scampering on like a terrier after a rat. When it came to rest, it was one yard ahead of Peter's ball, with both in perfect position to attack the pin. Peter also noticed Ben's perfectly balanced finish.

He was not fazed by Ben's shot. After all, they had just started. *This is going to be interesting*, he thought and his favorite business book, Sun Tzu's *Art of War*, came to mind—a book he recommended to his sales team. Sun Tzu wrote, "Do not attack an enemy's strengths, attack an enemy's weaknesses." Peter would just have to find Ben's weaknesses. His smile got wider and he concluded, *I am so going to enjoy this game. Finally, a real challenger.*

"Good shot, Ben. Nice to meet a fellow player. We're going to have fun," Peter said and actually meant it.

"Thanks Peter," said replied. "I'm a bit rusty but hopefully I can give you a game to remember," Ben smiled as they moved towards the golf cart.

Oh I will remember it all right, thought Peter, *I will.*

They got to their drives and got out of the cart to survey their shots. Ben took one look at the green, glanced at the tree tops, and pulled a club. Peter took a little longer and tried not to show his slight annoyance that Ben was now watching him. He had the club across his shoulders, both arms draped over each end, with a grin on his face.

"You look relaxed," remarked Peter.

"Why shouldn't I be?" said Ben. "I mean, it's only a game right, not life and death?"

Peter didn't respond, trying to hide the surprise he felt when Ben said what he did. *That's what the Scottish pro had told me when we played nine holes years ago.* The fact is that winning was life-and-death to Peter, especially since the state championship. *I'm going to have to watch this one*, he thought as he selected his iron and moved into the ball.

Once behind the ball, Peter surveyed the shot once more to commit it to memory. Peter wanted all the planning and decision making done behind and off the ball since he believed that once over the ball, one should just swing and not think.

The hole was a real Sunday-pin placement. From the tee, it was 135 yards to the front of the green and then 20 yards farther to the hole, two yards onto the top tier. The greenkeeper, in Peter's opinion, had an almost pathological hatred for golfers. He tried as often as possible to punish golfers for hacking up his hollowed turf. If your shot was short, it got you an uphill putt, up the tier. If your shot was long, it got you a chip from some snarly rough.

Peter took his eight iron and gripped an inch down the shaft to take a little distance off the club. He put the ball a little back in his stance since he wanted to run the ball up the green, trying to fly the ball all the way. This left little margin for error, but in Peter's mind, this would result in the best shot and put the pressure firmly on Ben. He swung the club and watched the ball fly on his intended line, land on the front of the green, and carry on, running towards the hole, slowly losing momentum. It reached the top tier of the green and slowly started its ascent upwards, until it reached the top and finally ran out of steam. It was five feet from the hole but in good position for a birdie. Peter felt this would surely be enough to win this hole and establish his superiority over Ben.

"Good shot, Peter," exclaimed Ben. "Nice to see that you were certainly not double-minded in that one," he added with a nod.

Strange, thought Peter, *that sounded like something my father might have said. What was it? 'A double-minded man is weak in all his ways.'* Peter was pretty sure it was a quote from the Bible. Peter had an amusing thought: *This guy must have given my father a call.*

Peter then watched Ben as he stepped up for his shot. He noticed that Ben had also gripped down on his eight iron and set the ball back in his stance, just as Peter had done.

Ben settled and then swung easily. The ball took off on a near identical path to Peter's, almost like Ben's ball was tracking on Peter's ball. The ball landed on the front of the green and released, rolling up the green, and eventually coming to a stop, two inches in front of Peter's ball.

"Good shot, Ben. Looks like you'll get a good read off my ball," he said with a trace of arrogance.

"Well, I don't mind a little help," said Ben. They drove up to the green in silence. Peter was trying to figure out what made this guy who was sat next to him tick. Peter suddenly thought, *Maybe I should try to get to know him? Then I can learn how to beat him?*

"So who taught you to play, Ben?" Peter inquired.

"Interesting question, Peter. Well let's see, putting and short game was Seve Ballesteros, irons was Ben Hogan, and woods was Sam Snead, with a little help from Greg Norman in that department too."

Peter put on his poker face even though he had never heard anyone say they had so many famous instructors. Peter was thinking, *This guy is so full of shit. Clearly Ben lives on a different planet from the rest of us,* but he played it cool. "Hummm. Three of your instructors have been deceased for a while," he said sarcastically. "The games changed since their days." Playing along with Ben's fantasy, he asked, "Why two wood instructors?"

Ben replied, "Well, Sam's got a fantastic action and is long, but Greg can hit fairways like a machine." Thankfully they were approaching the green because Peter was annoyed with Ben's pretence. *He expects me to believe all this?*

They walked up to their balls and Peter asked Ben to move the ball a putter-head's length away from his marker. Ben dutifully complied with his request. Peter's putt was not that difficult and he had been in almost the same position a month ago. One of the things that could be said for the greens keeper was his lack of imagination, for he maintained the same positions over the course of a year on a rotating basis. This was good for Peter and the better and more observant players, giving them a distinct advantage over a visiting player, which could prove very useful today in his game with Ben.

The putt was an inch on the topside of the hole, if struck medium firm. Peter knew this, so he set the blade of the putter behind the ball, took one last look at the hole, and putted. It tracked beautifully towards the hole and with the exact amount of break on the ball. It entered the hole, smack bang in the center and rattled gloriously in the cup. "Good putt, Peter," said Ben.

Peter didn't say anything, but raised his hand acknowledging the compliment.

Ben placed his ball back down, removed the marker, and checked his line. He then moved to the ball. If Ben did not move his ball back to the original position, having moved it at Peter's request, he would incur a two-shot penalty. That meant even if he holed his five-foot putt, he would be a five to Peter's three and Peter would win the hole and a thousand dollars. It was a no-brainer for Peter to stay quiet until Ben had putted, only then speak up. After all, this was war, and he was not cheating, just using the rules to his advantage.

Ben was about to place the putter behind the ball and was going to take one last look at the hole when he stopped and stood up. He turned to Peter and said, "I almost forgot something, didn't I?"

"Oh yes, you have to move the ball back to the correct position, don't you?" said Peter, feigning a shocked look. "Glad you remembered, Ben."

Ben smiled, "Yes I'm sure you would have said something before I putted if I had forgotten, wouldn't you?"

Peter didn't say anything but nodded slightly. "Anyway, all's well that ends well. Just tap that little one in and we're all square in threes." Peter was not the least bit embarrassed about Ben calling him out. Instead, he hoped the incident had rattled Ben just enough to make him miss the putt.

Ben re-marked the ball and set up to putt. Before the ball was halfway to the hole, Peter knew it was in. The ball dived into the hole like a rabbit. They had halved the hole in threes.

"Well," said Ben, "that was an interesting first hole. I think we learned that we both know how to play by the rules. Wouldn't you agree, Peter?" As he walked past Peter, he winked and gave him a pat on the shoulder. "Come on, let's get to the next hole."

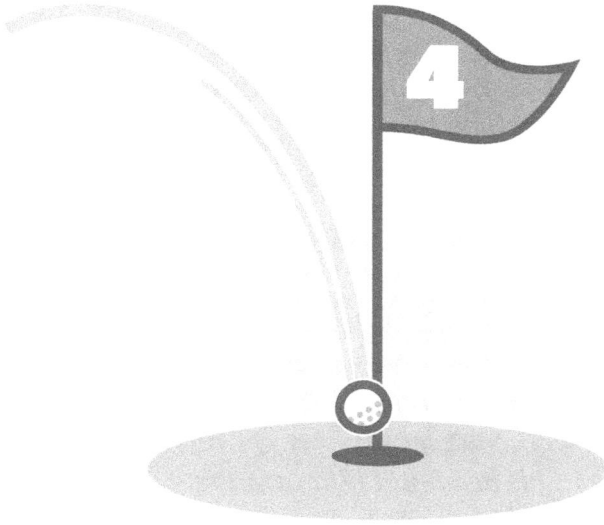

The Guest Can Play

Peter and Ben walked up to hole two, a short par four, 340 yards in length with a slight dogleg right. Though short in length, this hole was one where most members took their par and gratefully moved on to the next hole. The hole had a small pond in front of the tee purely to create an intimidation factor—by the designer's own admission. Off the tee, the path was 200 yards straight with bunkers waiting either side of the fairway to catch the player whose safety shot off the tee was errant.

After the bunkers, the fairway narrowed gradually up to the green, which was guarded on either side by deep bunkers. There was a fifteen-yard funnel that ran up to the green for those brave enough and long enough off the tee to try and reach it. Peter usually took a five iron and put it just over the bunkers at 200 yards, leaving him a pitching wedge to a nine iron to the green, depending on where his shot landed on the fairway, which sloped gently toward the front of the green.

Peter strode up to the tee box and pulled the cover off his driver. *No safe play is going to win this battle. I have to be bold and exert my authority over Ben. It's time this guy learned who's the boss of this course,* declared Peter to himself when Ben interrupted.

"I'm really enjoying the round so far. It's a lot of fun and this is a great course."

Peter was a little irked. He was the best player in the state and club champion, and he was playing a stranger for serious money, yet his opponent thought it was only casual fun. *Calm yourself. Don't let this guy get in your head. You're supposed to get in his head, not him in yours.*

Peter stood behind the ball and imagined the shot; he needed a medium height drive with a touch of fade. It was asking a lot under pressure, but Peter wasn't phased. Quite the opposite, he relished the chance to pull off the drive and establish his superiority. Happy with his shot plan, he moved into the ball, settled, took one last look, and drew the club back. Even before the club reached its peak, he felt balanced and powerful. The transition into the downswing was sublime and the impact was perfect.

Before the ball had gone 150 yards, Peter knew he had pulled the shot off. The ball screamed down the fairway and flew 200 yards over the bunkers. Then the fade he put on the ball kicked in and it landed at 300 yards and ran on finding the slot perfectly, coming to a stop seven feet underneath the hole—in perfect position for an eagle putt. He had taken the boldest option and pulled it off. In fact, it was the best drive he had ever played on this hole. He felt supreme at that moment. He was the man. If he was a lion, he would have roared. *Top that, Ben*, he thought.

"Great drive, Peter, and a beauty to watch," commented his opponent as he walked up to the tee box.

Peter noticed Ben also had his driver in his hand.

Interesting. Let's see what he can do. My drive must have rattled him, Peter concluded. Ben went through his usual pre-shot routine and settled over the ball. Peter watched like a hawk but when Ben started to swing, it was like he was watching in slow motion. Ben's motion was unhurried and effortless but deliberate at the same time. As the driver started to reach its zenith, Ben had already started rotating towards the target. At the top of his backswing, the club was pulled down by the rotation of his body, which had started in his feet.

Peter knew this is what all great players do, and every part of Ben's body was working together in the swing. It was in this moment, a half second before Ben made contact with the ball, that Peter knew in his heart Ben was not a good player—he was a great player. The sound of Ben's club meeting the ball took Peter back to the time he saw a top PGA tour pro at a company day. Peter's head whipped around to try and catch sight of his ball, but he only picked it up when it landed in the middle of the fifteen-yard slot as the ball ran up the green, coming to a halt only six feet below the hole. There was silence as both men savored the shot. Finally, Peter grudgingly but with great admiration, shook his head and confessed, "Fantastic shot!"

Ben said, "I enjoyed it too," and they moved off the tee and walked toward the golf cart.

Peter's brain was reeling. *I played one of the best shots of my life, only to see this son-of-a-bitch put a drive a foot inside my own on a 340-yard hole. Who the hell is this guy?* What was even stranger was the feeling that the better he played, the better Ben would play. It was as if he was fighting himself and not playing Ben. *Stop with the crazy thoughts and knuckle down or this man is going to eat your lunch.* Only an hour ago, Peter thought he was king of this course. By the second hole, he felt like he was being taken to school, humiliated in his own domain.

Stay calm, regroup, he thought. Then he started to feel angry. *Ben, you bastard, I'm not going down without a fight.* He was going to attack with everything he had. Whatever it took, Peter was going to win because he *always* won.

They drove in silence to the green. Peter was trying his best to compose his mind, assuring himself, *You can do this Peter. You are the best. You just have to outdo him and you can do that. No one has ever gotten the better of you without cheating, unless you lost on purpose and that isn't going to happen today.* Peter didn't care if this man had a contract in his pocket for a billion dollars' worth of Drexochem drugs. He was going to beat him at golf today, and nothing else mattered.

They reached the green and took out their putters. Ben marked his ball, which was a foot to one side of Peter's ball. He then moved off to the side to give Peter room to putt. Peter knew one thing for a fact: He had to hole this eagle putt to halve the hole. *I could be three under par after two holes and we will be all square. That's just crazy. It just doesn't happen in golf,* thought Peter, *and it has certainly never happened to me.*

Peter looked at his putt and could see it was uphill and would break a cup's width from the right-hand side of the cup. He placed the putter behind the ball and stroked it. The ball tracked dutifully towards the hole, taking the break Peter had seen, and dove into the hole perfectly for a two-shot eagle. "Yes," Peter shouted, louder than he had intended, but his desire to win was growing by the minute, like a malignant tumor he could not control..

"Good putt, Peter," said Ben, leave the ball. I'll get it for you in a minute." Ben placed his ball down and removed his marker. He looked at his putt briefly, set his putter behind the ball, and then stroked the ball as if it was all a foregone conclusion. The ball took the inch of break perfectly and joined Peter's ball in the hole. They had halved the hole with eagles.

This is crazy. I've never played this good and yet been all square in a match. Can I play any better? Peter felt a knot in his gut, for he knew the answer was no. Worse still, deep down he knew Ben could. For the first time in a long time, he felt an emotion he dreaded, that he had worked his entire adult life to overcome and eradicate, and that emotion was fear. He began to sweat, his calm demeanor totally gone. There was only one other time when he had experienced fear like this and he swore he would never experience it again. Peter wasn't ready to give in to the fear, despite feeling as if he had nothing left. He would go for it, as they say in Texas Hold 'em Poker. Peter was going to push all his chips into the center of the table; he was going all in.

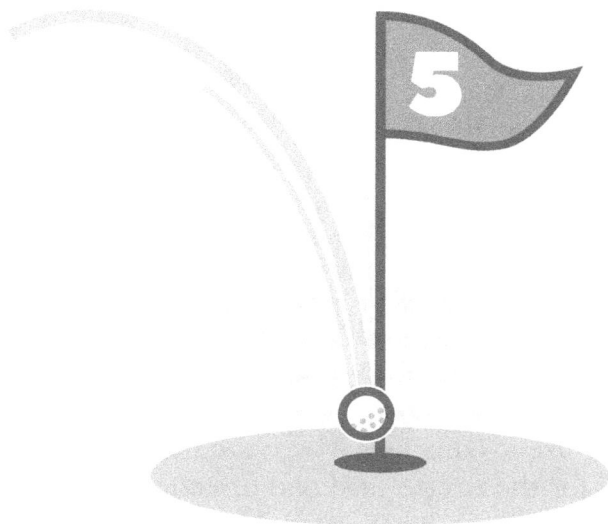

All In

The third hole was a tough, cleverly-designed par three of 165 yards from the championship tees. From the tee box, the green ran at a 45-degree angle to the left, which made the green look smaller, especially since there was a ten-yard elevation rise from tee box to green. Also, there was a swale of longer grass in a hollow that ran the length of the green, so a short shot meant recovery from the grass and no chance of spinning the ball as could happen from a sand bunker.

Although this hole was bunker-less, it was not defenseless, for the grass at the back of the green was also long. That made for a tricky shot if a player overshot the green. In short, this meant a player knew he had to hit the green to stand a chance at par, which was just the kind of pressure the designer had intended to put on the player as he stood on the tee. As Peter and Ben approached, they found the pin was right at the back, on the top of the second tier. The top tier itself was no more than 30 feet wide, so precision was the key to the first shot.

Peter took out his nine iron and stared at the hole, gleaning as much information as he could. There were trees surrounding the hole to a height of 60 feet, another cunning move by the designer since some players were lulled into a false sense of security, thinking the trees sheltered the hole from the wind. The trees did little to shelter the hole so the trick was to pay attention to the wind speed when choosing a club.

There was a water stop just before the hole and Peter had stopped to use it. This was where the better players had learned to feel for the wind speed and direction before going to the third hole's tee box. Peter noted the five-miles-per-hour wind on his right cheek, and then continued the drive to the tee box, happy that Ben had stayed in the cart. *That added information will give me a distinct advantage,* Ben assumed.

Peter decided to play a medium-height shot with a touch of draw that would have the ball land on the front tier and run up the green to the pin on the second and top tier. He only needed a three-quarter swing, given his strategy to fly the ball 135 yards to the front of the green where it would then run. It was a high risk shot but the reward would be high if he pulled it off. *Commit to the shot,* Peter coached himself.

Peter set the club behind the ball and swung, but as soon as he made contact, he knew he had pureed the ball. That would not have been a problem had this been a drive on a par five where ten or twenty extra yards is much appreciated, but this shot required finesse with a short iron and it usually spelled trouble if the ball landed halfway up the green ten yards farther than intended. Then it would run up the green like a thief with a handbag, not stopping for anyone.

Peter watched as his ball mounted the second tier with way too much pace and then went past the pin by twelve inches on the high side, finally scooting into the collar of rough guarding the side of the green. It came to rest two feet off the green in three-inch-thick grass. He was about eight feet from the pin with a tough pitch for even the best of players. Peter had gambled on this shot and gone all in, but it looked like he could lose it all.

"That was almost a great shot, Peter," commented Ben. "Just a bit too much adrenaline in it."

Peter realized Ben was right. He had not taken that into account and had played like a man possessed, missing one of the tangibles in the shot—his state of mind. He grimaced and muttered, "Guess so," as he cleared the tee box for Ben.

Ben also chose a nine iron, but he was taking almost dead aim for the pin. Ben placed the ball but stopped his setup and turned to Peter to explain, "It's going to be a high cut into that five-miles-per-hour wind, just in case you're wondering." Ben smiled and resumed his setup, leaving Peter with the knowledge that he had indeed noticed the wind.

It was as if he was seeing Ben swing for the first time, like he had blinders on during the first two holes. Watching Ben's swing was seeing perfection; it was hard to compute. Every movement flowed into the next movement seamlessly. This time Peter noted that Ben's effortless swing was the result of having no ego or fear. It sounded crazy but when he had watched tour players in the past, he could sense they were trying to control their fear.

Thus, as great as their swings were, he felt they were constantly trying or searching for their swing. This was not the case with Ben. Ben had no fear. Peter's dad had jokingly asked Peter once, "Can you imagine what it would be like to watch God swing a club?" Peter felt like that was what he was watching when Ben played. Peter had been fifteen at the time and not interested in another sermon from his dad, especially on the golf course.

Peter knew he was in trouble. His thoughts were

interrupted as he heard the pure sound of perfect contact on impact as the ball roared away on a ridiculously high trajectory with a hint of fade. The ball climbed until the energy of the impact, combined with the fade began to slowly dissipate until finally, dead center over the pin, the ball just dropped from the air, spent of all its energy and spin. The ball landed and bounced straight up two feet into the air and came to a stop, six inches from the hole.

The drive up to the green left Peter enough time to realize he was the puppy in this dog fight, not a good position to be in. When they walked onto the green, Ben's ball was so close that Peter picked it up and tossed it to Ben. "Superb birdie," Ben he said. Peter had brought two wedges and no putter onto the green because if he missed the pitch, he would lose the hole anyway. His ball was nestled in the grass and was going to require some force to get it up, but not too much because he didn't want distance. It had to rise quickly and land as softly as possible so it wouldn't run.

He dropped the 56-degree wedge on the fringe and went with the 60-degree wedge. He would use the bounce, and also have to lay it open and make a full swing, not Peter's favorite shot—but his only option. He settled into the shot, club face open, soft hands, and weight on the back foot to shallow the club on impact. When Peter swung, the ball popped up almost vertically and plopped onto the green, where it started trundling slowly towards the hole for the briefest of time. He thought he had pulled off the shot of the year until the ball jigged to the left and missed the hole by an inch, coming to rest eight inches past the hole.

He had lost the hole and even though he had seen it with his own eyes, he was still in shock. Ben scooped up the ball with the back of his putter and tossed it softly to him. "Great effort, Peter, so I'm one up, I believe. Let's see what hole four has in store for us."

As Ben turned to leave the green, Peter was faced with a terrible and painful truth: He had gone *all in* and lost; he was playing someone who was simply better than he was on his own course. *This cannot be happening, not right before the championship. This must be a nightmare and I'll wake up soon. I can't remember the last time I lost—at anything, let alone golf.* He shook his head recognising that this was no nightmare. It was real, very real.

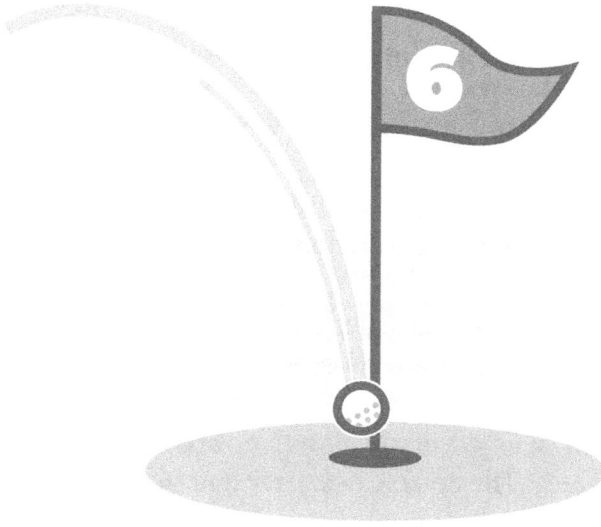

Pappa

"What business are you in, Peter?" Ben asked, as they drove to the next hole.

"I am in sales, drug sales," Peter replied. "I work for one of the big boys, Drexochem as the VP of sales. And what about your business?"

"Oh, I'm a conglomerate. I have shipping, communications, and humanitarian interests," Ben replied. It seemed to Peter like he was being slightly evasive in his answer.

"What's the name of your company?" Peter wanted to know, trying to solve this riddle of the man named Ben.

"Well, we're multinational and go by many names," Ben said, again leaving Peter with more questions than answers.

Peter decided the time for chit chat was done; he had a job ahead of him and needed to keep his head on golf. It was then that Ben dropped a bombshell.

"Peter, we're both successful businessmen, but at what

cost? I have been thinking about something someone once wrote that summarized the challenge with success: "What good is it for someone to gain the whole world, yet forfeit their soul?"

Peter almost drove the cart into the woods. *Now I know this guy has been talking to my dad. That is so something he would say while we played.*

"That's a pretty heavy question, Ben, and we have a lot more golf to play," Peter said, relieved they had arrived at the next hole.

Hole four was a classic par five, 560 yards from the championship tees. The course designer had been subtle in his design of the hole. Standing on the tee, all the golfer can see is four bunkers, two on either side of the fairway. Those bunkers were a clever means of making the golfer look where the designer wanted him to look, just like a magician who gets the audience to look at the right hand while the magic is carried out with the left hand.

The real danger was on each side of the fairway where parallel streams ran down each side. Forty yards from the green, the left hand stream cut across the fairway like a Scottish burn to join the right hand stream and create a pond. This pond skirted the green and wrapped around the right side and back of the green.

Peter parked and exited the cart. As he tugged the cover off his driver, Ben said, "Hey, Peter. You okay? You seem to be upset. If it's the money, we can just play for fun."

"Ben, I'm trying to concentrate and then you bring up some life philosophical question. You sound like you're my father who was always preaching to me?"

"Oh, I'm sorry," Ben said. "I didn't mean to upset you. I know how much you like to win."

"You just met me, Ben. You don't know me. We've never met," Peter said, but somehow he knew that wasn't quite accurate.

"I believe the tee is mine? Correct, Peter?"

Peter nodded his head so he would not have to state the obvious. Ben teed his ball up a little higher than normal. He placed his grip on the driver, took a look at his line, and then he moved into the ball, setting the club behind the ball. He took one last look and took the club back. Even though Peter was mad as hell, he noticed how relaxed Ben looked and how each movement blended perfectly with the other. This time, Peter noticed Ben was creating even more power in his back-swing. The transition was again flawless from backswing to downswing but the club seemed like a faint blur as it hurtled towards the ball.

The ball went screaming away with a sound of pure power and perfect contact all over it. Still forty feet in the air, the ball soared over the bunkers at 290 yards, coming down to earth at 340 yards and rolling out to a stop at 370 yards, leaving Ben only 190 to the green and 205 to the pin, which obviously put Ben in range for getting on in two at this par five.

This was not the tee shot of a plus four handicap. It was as good as anyone on tour could do and Peter knew it. Peter felt that if he clenched his teeth any tighter, he would snap his jaw. *I'm one down and this son-of-a-bitch is putting the hammer down even more. What are the limits of this man? What more is he capable of?* Peter took a deep breath and grudgingly uttered the words one more time, "Good shot," as he walked to the tee.

Peter teed up his ball and gathered himself as best he could. *I can't match Ben's shot so it's best not to even try. Play your game, not your opponent's,* he said to himself. *Hah, that was one of Dad's pieces of advice to me. My God, I must be struggling,* for he could not remember the last time he had taken advice from his Dad.

Peter focused on the shot he wanted to execute, which was a long drive past the bunkers at 290 yards if he was to have any chance of going for the green in two. *Focus, relax just your normal swing will do. Relax.* He started his swing but before he got to the top of his backswing, he knew something was off. He felt a little tight and out of balance. In truth, Peter was caught between two shots: the one he ought to play and the one he really wanted to play, which was to hit the ball as hard as he could to smash it to kingdom come. In essence, he was once again fighting with himself.

The club came down from the inside and Peter tried correcting it, as good players do, by holding the club off to protect against a hook, but he pushed the ball on a straight trajectory into the right hand bunker at 290 yards. "Sweet Jesus!" Peter exclaimed. He hoped the ball had not plugged, otherwise he would be sunk. His third shot would be from 150 yards plus, not exactly a great distance for making a birdie that he desperately needed considering Ben could be on the green in two. Peter turned and walked to the cart in silence, hoping Ben would not speak to him. He was not to be so fortunate.

"Peter," said Ben.

Peter stiffened. He wanted to lift his head to heaven and ask God to strike Ben mute.

Ben then said something that shocked Peter: "You know there's not much chance of the mute thing working out," Ben said with a knowing look. Peter's mouth dropped open; *How the hell could he know what I was thinking?*

"Anyway," Ben continued, "I know you don't like small talk but I was wondering why did you take up golf in the first place?"

What the heck. I'll play along. "My dad was a member at the local municipal course and he was the best player there. He held the course record and what kid doesn't want to hang out with his dad, so I used to tag along. He got a club for me and taught me to play while we talked about other stuff."

"What other stuff?"

Peter turned again to Ben and said, "God. He was always talking about God, morning, noon, and night. I used to like being out with him at first, but I grew tired of the God stuff. In the end, I started playing on my own or with other youngsters and then . . . ," Peter stopped talking, surprised at how much he had said and tried to turn the conversation away from himself. "Anyway, why did you start playing?"

Ben looked at him and said, "I've always played, Peter, even before there were courses, I played." Peter was about to ask for clarification when Ben said, "Your ball, I believe."

As he feared, Peter's ball was plugged—totally embedded in the sand. He walked around the area to get a good look but he knew he could look at it all day long but it would not change the fact that he was 260 yards from the front of the green and 270 yards to the pin. He had no choice but to blast out and play for position to have a good lie for his third shot.

Peter selected his nine iron and walked into the bunker. He put the ball back in his stance a bit since he wanted to put top spin on the ball so it would run up the fairway. That way Peter could use a short iron to put it in close to try and put some pressure on Ben. Peter took his stance and swung. He got the topspin he wanted and watched it hit the fairway 80 yards on and run like a thief with a handbag, finally stopping after a 120 yards and leaving 140 yards to the pin.

After Peter's shot, Ben walked toward his ball down the fairway. By the time Peter had raked the bunker and got into the cart, Ben was already at his ball, surveying the shot. Ben walked round the back of the cart and selected a seven iron. Peter thought, *This could be my chance. He hasn't got enough club to carry 215 yards with a seven iron. That's pushing it. This could definitely turn things around.*

Peter felt like there was a hope, like a beam of light had broken through the clouds. Ben settled over the ball in his usual fashion, which never deviated: grip the club, set the club, set the body, one last look, and swing. The swing was fluid and powerful but this time Peter felt Ben was applying even more force to the back of the ball. On contact, the ball screamed away as usual but on an impossibly high trajectory, so much so that Peter wondered if he had mishit it. A millisecond later, he realized Ben had played the shot like his dad's favorite player, Jack Nicklaus.

The ball clawed its way upwards and onwards until, as if through sheer exhaustion, it just fell from the sky like a shot bird, no life or spin left in it, just gravity letting it fall. It landed two feet from the pin and bounced once straight up into the air to come to rest in the exact place it had originally landed—two feet from the pin. *That isn't the shot of a mortal,* thought Peter. *What can you say after you've witnessed perfection?*

Peter whirled around to Ben and could no longer contain himself. "Who are you? he shouted at Ben. "No CEO I know can play like you. Not even PGA tour players can do that. Who are you, tell me?"

Ben looked Peter directly in the eye with a look that held Peter's attention. It was neither aggressive nor weak but held him captive without force, as if by expectation of what was to come. "When you were small, Peter, you knew me as Pappa. When your mom was sick, you talked to me with her but when she died, you left me. When you looked at me on the first tee and thought I reminded you of your father, you recognised me then. Peter, my question to you is 'Who do you think I am?'"

Peter's knees actually gave way like he had received a solid punch to his mid-section. His mind spun, he had a thousand emotions, and his heart was hammering in his chest like he had run a marathon. Peter was confused, desperately trying to stay in control and make sense of it all. *How did he know Mom was sick and died? There was only one person who I ever knew to be Pappa. It couldn't be, this is ridiculous. Could* *it be? Could this man standing before me be **Him?***

Peter could not bring himself to say it, hoping that not saying it would mean life stayed on the right side of crazy. Peter turned to walk to the cart hoping to stop the madness unfolding in front of him. He got to the cart and employed all the self-talk techniques he ever knew: *Peter, breathe. There's an explanation for this.* He steadied himself and stood breathing in and out, taking long deep breaths. Calm began to return.

Suddenly it came to him. *This is Brad's doing.* Peter always disliked him and never trusted him. He must have told Ben these things. Yes, Peter remembered that one day his dad had come to visit and had a long chat with Brad the pro. Yes, that must be it—a sick, cruel joke. But why? Why would Brad and his dad do something like this?

Peter drove to his ball. He didn't even bother waiting for Ben to get in so they could go the sixty yards or so to his ball. Driving to his ball was not easy. Even though he was sure he had the explanation, he was still shaken. His vision was almost tunnel-like, and nothing existed outside of the narrow path he was on to take his next shot.

Peter pulled up at his ball and strode to the back of the cart and there was Ben leaning on the side of the cart. "So you think you've figured it out?" he said. "That's so like you, Peter. No one pulls one over on you, do they?" Peter scowled but remained silent. "That's okay," Ben continued, "let's take it slowly with the answer to my question. There's plenty of time. Anyway, I've just loosened up now and I'm quite enjoying myself. It's your shot."

Peter tried to focus on his lie but realized that he couldn't block out the madness of a few moments ago when he had nearly been drawn in. Peter felt like he was slowly, but inevitably moving towards a vortex of confrontation. He would have to let Ben know he knew what he and Brad were doing, but he didn't want to give them the satisfaction of knowing he had been so rattled. His mind raced and he couldn't keep his composure.

"Damn! What's the point of carrying on," Peter exclaimed. "You're going to beat me anyway. Let's stop all the games, shall we?" said Peter. "It was a clever thing you and Brad did, and you, well it was perfect what you did back there. You nearly had me believing . . ."

"Believing what?" said Ben. "It's been a while since you've believed anything, Peter."

"It doesn't matter. I get it. Brad wanted to teach me a lesson, I know people think I'm arrogant, but I earned where I am. I deserve what I have."

"You did, yes, you did," Ben agreed.

"I worked hard, I made the targets, I brought in the big clients and I deserve to be where I am."

"Right again, Peter. You did do all those things but do you really think you did them on your own? The rain falls on the just and the unjust doesn't it?" Ben said.

Peter was thrown off guard again. His dad loved to say that nothing was by our own hands or simple good luck. It was the grace of God. Suddenly Peter felt anger like he had not felt since the state tournament or when his mother died. *How could he? How could my dad do this?*

Ben interrupted his train of thought. "This has nothing to do with your dad."

"How did you . . .?" Peter started to ask but could not finish. *How did Ben know what he was thinking like that?* His mind was searching for an explanation. *No, it was a sick, cruel joke; it couldn't be.*

Ben pressed in. "Do you really think your dad could play a joke like this on you? You know your dad's a quiet man. He doesn't tell anyone his business, and as much as you dislike Brad, you know there is no way he spoke to me about you. So that leaves only one real explanation doesn't it, Peter?" said

Ben. "Clock's ticking, Peter, as your mom would say, 'Time is precious.'"

Peter could no longer stand. He was on his knees searching, wracking his brain for an explanation other than the fact that Ben was God himself. Ben put his hand on Peter's shoulder. All of a sudden it became crystal clear. His breathing slowed and he stood up, coming face-to-face with Ben. He knew that face, he knew that touch. Suddenly, there was light, the light he did not want. He had been happy in the dark. He was happiest being alone, especially since his mother, his best friend, and the smartest woman he had ever known, had left him to fend for himself.

PART TWO

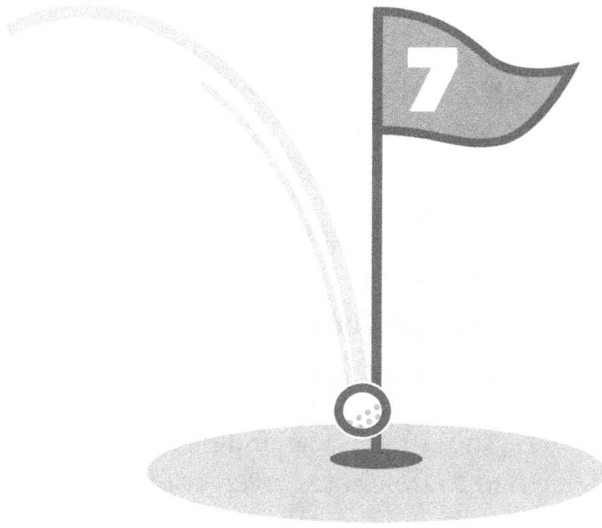

Mom

Peter walked into the house and his mother looked up from her paper. "How's my Petey?" Peter grinned even though he hated being called Petey. The good news is his mother had stopped calling him "little" Petey. Peter knew better than to say anything to her. His father had warned him on numerous occasions that despite his mother being smarter than your average genius, she was a Mom at heart and that was her way of showing it. Peter wondered, *Why the heck did Mom marry Dad if she was so smart?*

Peter's relationship with his mother was not a typical one. His mom did not spend all her time in the kitchen like his friend's mom's. His mom had mastered the art of the 30-minute meal. Also, whose mom spent hours every day reading the *Wall Street Journal* or books on economics? She would take copious notes in one of her many notebooks piled in the corner of the family room, much to his father's annoyance.

His father had brought it up once, threatening to throw them out, to which his mom replied ever so sweetly, "They're my hobby, Honey, and if you throw them out, I will have to take up golf with you." Peter's father backed off and never raised the subject again. He warned Peter to pick his battles carefully. No doubt his mother had played a part in his dad learning that truth.

Peter was an only child, and in his mind, he should have been indulged like the others he knew who were an only child. Sadly, this was not the case. His parents believed in "training him up in the way he should go," a saying he later learned was from the Bible. He had to do chores, even cooking a meal for everyone on Saturdays, and he wasn't chauffeured around everywhere. He had to ride his bike if he wanted to go someplace.

Peter remembered saying to his mom one Saturday that he spent more time in the kitchen than she did. She responded with a sly grin, "That's because you're not organised like me. With practice, you'll get faster." She playfully pinched his cheek and went back to her paper. Oh yes, he thought, *pick your battles*, and he went back to thickening the gravy.

When Peter walked in, his mom was sitting at the kitchen table reading and making notes. "How was school, Petey? What did you learn today?" Peter's mom had always been interested in his schooling but now that he was 16 and thinking about what was next, his mom was even more interested.

Peter put down his backpack, thought carefully about his response, then blurted out, "To be honest, I'm beginning to feel like it's all a waste of time. I'm not sure I want to go to university. I had statistics today and not only was it boring but I can't see any use for it in the real world." As far as Peter was concerned, anything that didn't directly relate to getting rich was a waste of effort.

His mother kept reading and didn't say anything but Peter thought, *Oh no, I feel another lesson coming.*

"I know you want to be rich one day," she began, "but let's consider how that can happen. Say you had an airline business. How do you make money?"

"You sell tickets to take people where they want to go, and you need to sell enough tickets to cover your costs and expenses so you can make a profit," Peter said.

"Great. Now assume you've charged the highest price possible for your tickets, because you want to be cost competitive in comparison to your competitors. How else can you increase your profits?"

Peter thought for a minute. "If I can't increase the price of the tickets, I'll have to reduce my costs."

"Very good. Assume you have reduced your costs and made your operation as efficient as possible, what else could you do to increase profit?"

"I can't, unless I can sell more tickets. But there is only so much space on the plane."

"Ahhh," said his mom. "You looked at binomial distribution in statistics, right?"

Peter frowned and replied, "I can't remember."

"Well, it's simply a distribution of the frequency of possible numbers of successful outcomes in a given number of trials in each, of which there is the same probability of success."

Peter was getting bored and interrupted, "But what does . . . ?"

"Hold on, I'm coming to it," she said. "If you were to take groups of passengers over a period of time and calculated the binomial distribution to show how many passengers show up for their flight, as opposed to canceling them, you could predict the probability of people showing up. That means you could oversell tickets and make more money."

With that, his mom launched into a more in-depth explanation of statistics with many other examples of its application. If Peter was not eating egg rolls from last night's dinner, he would not have hung around for the lesson. He had already spent the day in school.

Peter looked at his watch and two hours had gone by. He had to admit that his mother had found a real-world use for statistics. This was his mother all over. Whenever she asked a question, it was because she was really interested in the answer. And she loved being asked an interesting and challenging question. Peter's father often said, "Your mother has a V-8 engine for a brain. Try not to ask a four-cylinder question."

Despite Peter's reticence about going to university after high school, he was bright and hated to fail at anything, so he was a focused student. His mother often said, "Petey, time is a precious gift from God, so use it wisely." He had to admit that their house was a case study in that principle. His mom always had multiple activities going on but nothing as mundane as Tupperware parties or watching daytime television dramas. Theirs was a house where laughter, learning, and serious conversation went hand-in-hand. There was always something going on, be it a Bible study group at their house (usually every Wednesday), a summer cook out with close friends and family (he and Dad did the cooking), or the financial help group his mom and dad had started and led through the church.

Peter felt loved and challenged by his parents and they gave him space to explore the world through books, and the occasional trip, mainly connected with church missions. He also loved hearing about the places his parent's church friends had visited, some of the remotest areas on the planet as far as he was concerned. Yes, he was frustrated with his dad because in his mind he wasn't a go-getter or the kind of successful guy he admired and wanted to be, but he could see his dad had a peace that few fathers he met had. And his mom? Well, she was nothing short of brilliant, if not a bit eccentric.

Then the day came that changed the dynamics of his

family forever. As he came home from school, he put his backpack down and went into the kitchen where his mom was usually sitting, reading, and waiting to grill him on his day. This time, she wasn't there.

She was in the family room where his dad sat next to her on the settee. Peter was surprised to see his dad home so early. As Peter walked in, both his mother and father looked up and in an instant Peter realized that nothing in their home was ever going to be the same. His mother smiled weakly and said, "Sit down, Peter, I have something to tell you." Peter, stiffened because she never called him Peter unless he was in trouble or it was serious.

"Peter," his mother began, "you're nearly a man. You'll be off to university soon so I'm just going to say what I have to say. I've got cancer. There's no easy way to say it." He saw his father grimace and he felt confused, like an eight-year-old boy who had gotten lost in the shopping mall. *What am I supposed to say?* He ran to his mother and hugged her and they just stayed that way for a long while. Peter was crying as she stroked his head, saying the words he didn't believe: "It's going to be all right, Peter."

Looking up, he looked her straight in her eyes and fighting back tears, he asked, "Are you sure, Mom? Are you sure?"

"Yes, because God's in control; He's got this," and she said it with such confidence and joy that Peter instantly believed her. He felt a rush of relief that whatever form of cancer she had, it was not going to affect his mother or their family. Peter let out a sigh of relief that his mother was going to be all right.

As the weeks and months went by, things did not get better for his mother. Peter watched as her health slowly deteriorated. His parents tried to carry on as normal but it could never be normal with the endless hospital visits, surgery, and then chemotherapy, which kept his mother in the hospital for weeks. When she came home, she was too sick to function, and Peter cooked on more than just Saturdays.

His mom did seem to turn a corner for a while but she was still weak, joking, "Well, at least my hair is growing back. Your dad always did like it short." *That was Mom*, thought Peter, *a fighter*.

Peter noticed that the Bible study group spent a long time praying for his mom rather than studying as before. Peter felt emboldened enough to pray with his mother, something he had not done since he was a young child. He realized he actually missed their chats with Pappa, as they had called God when Peter was a tyke. The time he and his mom spent with Pappa really cheered her up and that made Peter happy too.

Time marched on and despite some positive signs, it was clear the cancer was not gone. One day, the principal called Peter out of class. This was the day he had secretly feared, almost forgetting his bag in a panic when he answered the call. He followed the principal out to the car park where Peter's dad was waiting. His dad tried to sound normal, but he explained, "Your mother's very unwell and so the ambulance had to come and take her to hospital. We need to go there now," he said. He put a hand on Peter's shoulder and gave it a reassuring squeeze, which was difficult because he had no reassurance himself. Peter reached up and touched his hand, adding, "It's okay, Dad. It's going to be fine. Mom said so."

They drove the rest of the way to the hospital in silence. Peter had felt in control and was telling himself it was going to be fine, but in the silence, doubt began to creep in. Finally, Peter had to ask, "Dad, she is going to be all right, isn't she?" Peter saw his father grip the steering wheel tightly holding in as much emotion as he could. Then he heard him say almost in a whisper, "I don't know, Peter, only God knows."

They entered the hospital and were greeted by the smell

that only hospitals have, getting a whiff of disinfectant with a hint of illness. How illness could have a smell seemed strange, but it was there, and Peter would never forget it. They went straight to reception and the nurse took them to the room his mother was in. She was hooked up to all kinds of tubes and monitors.

Peter heard the nurse tell his father, "She's comfortable, but that's all we can do." Peter was shocked. His mom looked so frail with a drip in her arm that Peter later learned was morphine. He had said goodbye to his mother before going to school that morning and he remembered thinking she was looking better for the first time in months, more like her old self. She had even managed to make him pancakes with maple syrup, his favorite breakfast of all time. All that was now a distant memory watching his mother lying there.

As Peter and his dad came closer, she smiled weakly at them. "Well, my men are here, about time," she said. They sat down next to her, his dad on one side of the bed and Peter on the other, each holding a hand. They stayed in this position for what seemed hours, neither Peter nor his dad moving or looking away as his mom drifted in and out of consciousness. Then finally she opened her eyes and looked at them both and said, "I love you both so much."

Then she shut her eyes again and a minute later Peter felt the life leave his mother. He looked at his father and they both knew his mother was gone. His father's face contorted into a mask of grief as he put his head on his wife's hand and sobbed. Peter had never seen his dad like this and at first he didn't know what to do. Then he got up and came to the other side of the bed where his father was sobbing. He put his hand on his shoulder, and any composure Peter had left him as he crumpled over his father and hugged him for dear life as they cried tears of sadness. Then came the anger, not from his dad but from Peter.

Through sobs, Peter spat out, "What kind of God allows this? She believed in him; He was supposed to help her. What's real is that He's not real and now she's dead."

Peter's dad managed to get up and cradle his son. He held him tightly, trying to absorb Peter's pain. Through tears and sobs, he said, "It will be okay, Peter. She's in a better place." He knew it was not the time to explain why God hadn't saved his wife. Truth be told, he would not have known what to say.

Peter and his dad left the hospital. Doctor Franks, his mom's doctor, actually came to visit them, telling them how amazed he had been at the way Peter's mother had handled her illness. He had never seen a patient go past six months with such an advanced stage of cancer, so how she made it to 13 months was anybody's guess. He said he was also impressed by her faith. Despite the severity of her case, she never stopped trusting God. Doctor Franks wanted Peter and his dad to know that because of Peter's mom, he had started attending church again.

For Peter and his dad, the funeral was a blur. The months that followed were a whirlwind of emotions for both of them. It was made bearable by the people regularly coming round in acts of support, which meant that he and his dad had little time alone. People were well-meaning with their sympathy but he felt like they were hollow, as if speaking to a child who had lost a sports race. He knew they didn't know what to say really, but the truth was he had lost and lost big time. God had not been there for him or his mom. Inside he was furious. Never again would Peter pray or ask God for anything. In the future, he would rely on himself and his efforts, because that way he could never be let down or lose big again—ever.

Peter's pleasant memory was interrupted by a later one, and his brief happiness turned to sadness when he remembered when and why he had stopped playing golf with his father. It was all because of the party that opened his eyes to an entirely different world. That event opened Peter's eyes to the life he wanted, but before then, never even knew it existed. It was a high school party for a class friend named John who lived in a swanky new estate. The party was shortly after his mother's death. John was new to their town and his dad worked in insurance whereas most of the other father's Peter knew worked in the trades as plumbers, carpenters, or electricians.

Peter realized the small suburb he grew up in was changing but his father wasn't. New and more expensive houses were being built to accommodate the influx of middle-class professionals who had decided the forty-minute commute to their work in the city was more desirable than living in that busy, smog-filled metropolis. Living where Peter had lived all his life meant those professionals could enjoy the countryside and have the quality time they worked hard all week to afford.

The phrase quality time made Peter's father smile and shake his head. His view was that if you're only living to be happy on weekends, then something was wrong with your life. Peter's dad seemed to have a different perspective than most people and it was only getting worse in Peter's mind.

At the party, Peter saw another way of living, one he knew about but had never paid much attention to. He decided what he wanted more than anything else was money and power so he could have the things that John's family had. He hated the little house his father had built on their half-acre plot with the help of his church friends so he would have no mortgage. If he had a dollar for every time his father told him "debt does not live in this house," he would have been wealthy before his sixteenth birthday.

When Peter got to John's house, he saw the gleaming BMW in the driveway. To top it all off, they had a pool. He was mesmerised by the splendour on show. Everything was perfect, from the manicured lawns to the elegant house fronts.

It was like comparing night and day to the rest of the town, not to mention his home. This was the world he should have been born into. Since he was not born into it, he decided he was going to create it.

Peter wanted to attend university to honor his mother's wishes. His dad had wanted him to study economics so he could become an economist and help put the country back on the straight and narrow. Peter wanted to major in economics but of a different kind. Peter wanted to earn serious money when he was out of school. Increasingly, he and his father disagreed, at first calmly, but increasingly there was tension and anger.

Peter went off to university and in a sense, never came back home. He rejected not only his father's values and lifestyle, but his father as well. They stayed in touch, but Peter kept him at arm's length. He didn't want to hear about God or heaven, and especially the Bible. Peter decided he was the master of his own fate. He didn't need help to get everything he desired.

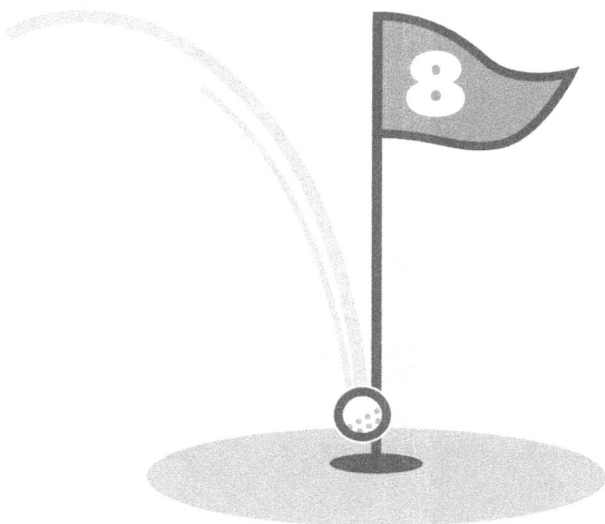

Golfing With God

Peter began to yell angrily at Ben. "What have you come here for? What do you want?"

Ben replied, "I came to help you, to set you free."

"Free from what? I don't want to be free. I like my life. I like where it's at."

"But Peter, if you're honest . . ."

"Honest?" snapped Peter. "I am honest. I don't cheat. I don't lie," but at that, Peter stopped and they both knew why.

"At golf you don't do those things, but how about the rest of your life, Peter?" Peter had been caught in a lie, the very thing he said he did not do.

"And when you promise a delivery of drugs and you know the delivery date cannot be met? Is that a lie?"

"All right, Ben, you caught me. Go ahead punish me some more, like you did at the tournament. Go ahead, maybe you want to take my wife this time?" Peter blurted out.

61

"Whoa, Peter," Ben responded. "Those are some pretty heavy accusations."

Peter was into it now, years of frustration and anger spewing forth toward the being he blamed for his life's circumstances.

"I suppose since I lied, you're going to take away my job?"

"No, Peter, I gave you that job. I won't take it away."

"You gave me that job?"

"I did. It was an answer to your mother's prayer that you be taken care of after she was gone."

That comment stopped Peter in his tracks. "My mother prayed for this job?"

"Oh yes, and a whole lot more. She knew you wanted to have money, so she prayed and I provided. I've done a pretty good job, don't you think?"

Peter suddenly realized they were playing on a usually busy course but there were no other people playing behind them.

"Don't worry, Peter," Ben interjected. "I made sure no one else would be here today so we could have the time we needed to talk. I knew I would find you here. In fact, I find and talk to many people out here. I laugh when they say on a Sunday, 'I will be worshiping on the course today.' I'm happy to meet them here."

Peter looked for a seat but there wasn't one, only the golf cart. He retreated there with Ben following.

"Peter, I know you want to win today. You want to win every day. I am here to prove to you that you don't have to win at other's expense. And you don't have to win it all to be happy."

"You've not only been fighting yourself, Peter, you have been fighting me. Today, you sensed there was something different about me, but you didn't care. You saw me as another chump to beat."

Peter replied softly, "You're right, but now you're here to get even."

"Get even?" Ben exclaimed. "You think I want to get even? I am not here to get even. I'm here to help."

"How can you help me?"

"I'm here to show you that you don't have to beat me, and that I'm not out to get you. I am here to show you that what you have seen today—how I've played, my swing, my command can all be yours, if you do it like I do, not in your own way or power."

"I don't get it," Peter said in a rare admission of weakness.

"Would you like to play this next shot as I see it. Feel it as I feel it?"

"What do you mean?" Peter said with a trace of confusion. "Are you saying I can actually play the shot as you do?"

Ben laughed, "I mean just the shot. I'm not giving you the power to part the Red Sea. I'm saying just play this one shot as I would, without any limitations—no fear, anxiety, or exertion, and with love instead of anger.

Peter asked, "Why would you do that? I don't even have a faith in . . . "

"Peter," Ben interrupted, "the funny thing is your faith is huge. The problem is it's faith in the church of me, myself, and I. You're dead right to say you have no faith in me. You have faith only in what you can do for yourself, with no one's help."

"You have a choice; play this shot with faith in you—and how's that been working out for you?—or try a different way and put your faith in me. If you spend 30 seconds playing a shot the way I do, your old way will feel like a cheap suit! It's your call. I mean you have free will and all," said Ben with a wry smile.

Peter paused for a moment—trying to make sense of it all. "Okay, Ben. What the hell, er the heck, sorry, have I got to lose? I'll try it your way."

Peter stood there waiting for his lesson, then Ben began. "It starts when you pick the club up. It will end when you put it down. Go ahead, Peter, your shot. Remember what you saw me do and imitate it"

Peter's hand hovered over his bag, looking at the wedge but not wanting to touch it, like it was a snake. Everything around him looked the same, but he felt like the man who stood on the edge of a lovely field suspecting it was a mine field. Peter was aware that what he was about to do could be life changing, but he wasn't sure he wanted his life to change. He had been happy with his lot.

Peter stood with the wedge in hand and looked at the world through new eyes, thinking, *My God, I'm playing golf with God! No wonder he reminded me of my father!* What he was seeing and feeling was so different from the world he had been looking at less than a minute ago. What he saw was exactly the same as before, but it was all new. Suddenly the grass on the fairway was linked to the trees in the woods, which in turn were linked to the green 140 yards in the distance. This fact brought the world to life like he had never seen or felt it before. He struggled to remain standing, that's how overcome he was with emotions from his new perspective on life.

Peter felt a hand on his shoulder and a calm strength flowed through him. He turned and saw Ben with his arm resting on his shoulder with a gentle smile on his face. He was relieved to see him there, like the time as a young child when he had fallen into a stream only to have his father's strong hands pluck him up and save him. It was an uneasy feeling but he needed it and so did not fight it. "Are you okay, Peter?" Ben asked.

"Not really," Peter replied truthfully, "I'm not used to, you know, like . . ." but before he could get the words out, Ben finished the sentence for him, ". . . not used to **not** being in control? Just relax, Peter," and Peter exhaled and loosened his shoulders. Peter entered into the new world he saw before him and knew he must look like a child on his first trip to Disney World.

Peter could feel the slight breeze on his cheek but he could also sense the shot forming in his mind. He could see the trajectory and the shape, but the strangest thing was that his motivation had changed. He felt calm and relaxed, like he hadn't felt in years and it hit him: He was free from anger. Peter realized he had been angry for a long time, so long he had forgotten what it was he felt like to be content and relaxed.

Strangest of all, he felt love, and just considering the word blew his mind but it was true. What did love have to do with playing golf? He felt an all-encompassing love for everything around him. It made him feel lighter because he was not carrying his usual loads of anger, resentment, and jealously to name a few. He felt like he had lost weight, and it was wonderful to be so focused without the pressure of having to succeed.

Peter saw a thousand possible ways to play the shot but saw only one clearly and picked it like one would pick a shirt from the rack. He settled over the ball, took one last look, and swung the club. He instinctively knew from the time the club was waist high that it was good. As he transitioned into the downswing, he felt the club being pulled to the ball and then the feeling of impact and compression. The ball roared away on a low-to-high trajectory with a hint of draw to counter the breeze playing across the hole. Peter felt euphoric, never having enjoyed a shot so much and it had not even landed.

When the ball landed in the cup, jamming itself in between the flag and the hole, he was not surprised, elated, or pumped because those feelings were unnecessary. He realized he had submitted his usual desires and wants for something pure—a feeling he could not really explain but it felt like pure joy. It was bizarre that he had gotten all that from a 140-yard golf shot.

Before he put his club back into his bag, he immediately felt the old feelings of anger and bitterness resurface. The colors faded and he no longer felt connected to everything. In short, he felt alone. It struck him that he was one unhappy man—but the man, or God, next to him held the key to Peter seeing, feeling, and living his life differently. He wasn't sure he really *wanted* to change but he knew he *needed* to change.

"That was impressive—an eagle from 140 yards," Ben commented.

"You set me up. You knew that to see it as you see it would involve a lot more than just hitting a white ball into the hole. You . . ."

Before he could finish, Ben raised his hand and Peter stopped. "I remember asking if you wanted to play this shot as I see it. You seized that chance because earlier, your desire to beat me blinded you to the possibilities. Peter, don't blame me for anything you felt or saw. It's time you faced your mistakes. My goodness, you sound like Adam."

Ben continued, "Peter, your desire to win and be the best has made you do and become some ugly things. On that shot, you got a chance to feel life for what it really is, not for what you have made it to be." Winking at him, Ben said, "Now if you will excuse me, I have a putt to make."

Peter was speechless all the way to the green. Ben hopped out of the cart, strode up to his ball, marked it, cleaned it, and then said to Peter, "Uh, could you remove the flag please?" Ben wasted no time setting his putter behind the ball and nonchalantly stroked the ball into the hole, plum center. "I do believe I am one up. Do you want to continue, Peter?"

"Do I have a choice" asked Peter sarcastically.

"Oh, you do, Peter, you always have a choice, which is why I gave you the gift of free will. That's how I made you," and with that amazing statement, the two players moved on to the next hole.

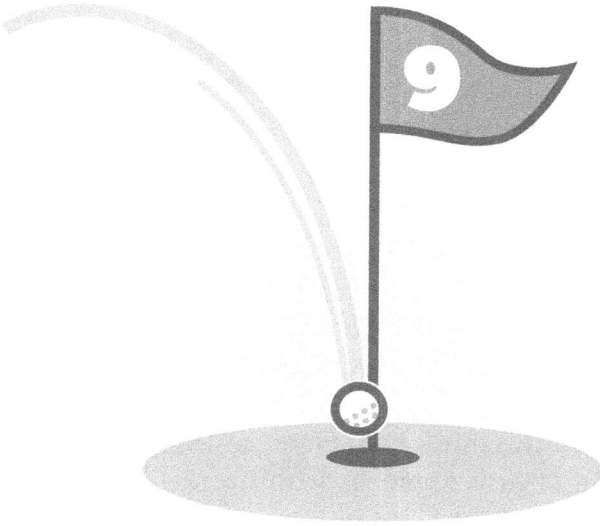

Learning to Let Go

Hole five was a straightaway par four of 400 yards with a stream and trees on the left and right. There was only one bunker on the hole in front of the green and a pond on the left back of the green. Peter chose his three wood and Ben his one iron and they walked up the steps to the tee box. "I have a question to ask you, Peter. Why did you take up golf?"

"Why ask me, Ben? You know the answer."

"Yes, that's correct, but I want to hear you say it."

"I wanted to spend time with my father because I loved being around him and I looked up to him. He was always helping me learn about life and was fun to be with."

Ben responded, "Did your father stop trying to help you, Peter, or did you stop listening to his advice?"

Peter did not answer and Ben did not press him for one. Once again, Peter was feeling emotions he had not felt for years. *How could I have lost his way so completely?*

Ben interrupted again with a hand on his shoulder and Peter felt the calm return. "A ship that goes off course is not lost, it's just off course, I came to get you back on course," Ben said. "If you will let me, I will help you. You think you have everything you want, but do you really?" Then Ben switched gears and said, "My shot I believe."

Peter's mind was muddled again with defensive thoughts. *I was having a great life until this guy turned up. Is he really God? Was my last shot just a fluke? Do I really care about any of this?*

"I am who you think I am Peter, and you weren't having such a great life. It was a veneer with no real substance. You just did a damn good job of hiding it, self-medicating with an overabundance of wine and work, both of which don't help to change the fact you feel pain and no number of gadgets or toys are going to make go away."

"That's easy for you to say," Peter said defensively.

Ben sighed and said, "A famous leader once said: 'Projects undreamed of by past generations will absorb our immediate descendants, comforts, activities, amenities, pleasures will crowd upon them, but their hearts will ache and their lives will be barren, if they have not a vision above material things.' Do you know who said that?"

"No," Peter replied.

"It was Prime Minister Winston Churchill, and like many of you, he had knowledge of truth from my Word without even realising it."

"What do you mean?" asked Peter.

"Well," Ben said, "when you get a chance, check out Luke's gospel, chapter twelve, verse fifteen. Now, may I proceed with my shot?" Ben asked, without waiting for an answer.

Peter asked Ben to repeat the Bible reference and wrote it on the back of his scorecard. Then he inquired, "Should I call you God or can I call you Ben?" Ben didn't answer, and

Peter added, "I'm going to lose, aren't I?"

"You can call me Ben, and yes, you are going to lose, but not in the way you think."

Ben turned to his teed-up ball and looked at the hole, grinning as he took his grip and placed the one iron behind the ball. Peter wondered why Ben had chosen a one iron. Ben started his swing and this time, Peter was watching not for faults but for help. Ben's swing started with a slight forward push of his hands towards the ball and the rest was a perfect combination of tempo, balance, and grace.

The club was in the perfect plain coming down and the impact of iron and ball was superb. The ball took off on a low and hissing flight heading towards the right-hand side of the fairway. Peter could see the draw spin having its effect on the ball, which even at its peak height never went above the tree height of 50 feet. The ball drew back to the center of the fairway and landed at 250 yards with its running shoes on, coming to rest on the left hand side of the fairway 300 yards from the tee. That left the perfect angle, 100 yards to the front edge of the green to a pin that was 15 yards farther back. *How do I follow that?*

Ben turned to him and replied, "You don't try to follow that, Peter, but you learn from it to help you play your own shot." Ben was trying to help him but Peter was not getting it, even though he had played this hole many times, often making the same mistakes. Peter stuck with his club choice and settled on the shot to be played. He was happy with what he had visualised—to play the ball down the right side with a hint of draw to bring it to the left side of the fairway for the best angle to the green, just like Ben had achieved but doing it Peter's way.

Peter took his stance and had one last look. The swing was good and the ball took off on a higher trajectory than Ben's, ten feet above the tree line. Peter waited for the draw spin to kick in but it didn't. It just kept following a straight line. *Turn ball, turn. Why isn't it turning?* he heard himself saying, but the ball was not listening. The ball landed at 275 yards off the tee in the semi-rough, taking one small hop and coming to rest 280 yards off the tee and 135 yards from the flag and on the wrong side of the fairway in the first cut of rough.

"Ok, Ben," said Peter with an air of resignation, "what didn't I learn that I should have on that shot?"

"One thing is if you keep doing the same thing but expect different results, you are in for disappointment. You had already made your mind up and that prevented you from being open to receive the help I was giving you. This hole changes every day because of the wind, rain, other conditions, and experience can't always help you."

"Often, Peter, you leave no room for change. You are the judge and jury and your decisions are final. My question to you is what will it take for you to change? You know I'm God, you saw me hit a perfect tee shot on this hole, and yet to you, it didn't make sense to copy me, even if what I'm doing works."

Peter had to admit Ben was right but wasn't going to say so. *He knows what I'm thinking anyway.*

Ben went on, "Life is like golf. We find a good teacher, take lessons, learn the correct way to play, and go out and do it."

Peter didn't know how to respond except to say, "Boy, I feel pretty stupid right now."

Ben laughed and replied, "Stupid I can work with but arrogant and stubborn are more difficult. Let's go to the tee and try it a different way. What do you think? It's only your life we're talking about. Plus, you're a thousand down and I take it you would like to stop the bleeding."

How can I when you birdie every hole," Peter said, realizing that he was joking with God and God wasn't put off.

When They arrived at Peter's tee shot, Peter said, "What should I do?"

"Hummm, there are always consequences to our decisions, and people usually turn to me when their shots go awry. The question is not 'what should I do?' but rather 'what can I do within the boundaries of the fairway?' You know good golf is played when you don't follow a bad shot with another bad shot. So I would aim for the flag except that it will run on because you can't put any spin on the ball. The ball will roll out 10 to 15 yards, leaving you two putts for par."

"Couldn't I aim for the front of the green and let the ball run out nearer the hole?" Peter asked, still hoping to find a way on his own.

"What if the ball really flies from that lie and you end up in the pond that is left rear of the green? Remember what your dad used to say?"

"Yes, it's greed and ego that gets us in a downward spiral on the course and in life."

"I taught him that," Ben said without a trace of pride.

Peter pulled the wedge and lined up the shot, placing his grip on the club and moving into the ball to take his shot. He settled over the ball and swung. The ball, as expected, flew out of the semi-rough like it was a turbo-charged laser heading for the flag, which it missed by a foot. It landed and ran on, ending up 12 yards past the flag in a position where two putts were possible with an outside chance of a birdie three.

"Good shot," said Ben who walked the twenty-five yards or so to his ball. Ben moved into his ball and settled over it. The swing was a three-quarter swing, beautifully balanced and exuding tempo. The ball took off lower but with a ton of spin (better players realize that a low shot can have more spin than a high one if executed properly). The ball honed in on the flag like it was radio controlled, hit the green three yards short of the flag, bounced forward one-and-a-half yards, then the spin made it dig its heel in and stop four-and-a-half feet from the hole, leaving a slightly uphill birdie putt.

"Wow," Peter exclaimed, "a perfect shot."

As they rode to the green, Peter said, "You really are giving me lots of leeway as I play, aren't you? I mean, you aren't forcing me to do what you suggest, even though it's the best way to play. When you let me see everything as you see it during my wedge shot, I have to say the shot was not the high point. It was the first time in a long time I felt love, peace, and joy all at the same time. I want to feel that again, I didn't realize how angry I am most of the time."

"And how's that working out for you?" Ben asked.

"Not so good, not so good at all," Peter replied.

Ben knowingly shook his head and said, "Following me is not like pick-and-mix at the candy counter. You can't leave out some things and take others. That's not how it works, though many who profess to follow me do just that. I will explain more if you want but first, let's finish this hole."

They marked their balls and Peter shouted across to Ben, "You know I haven't given up on beating you yet!" Ben waved and nodded that he heard the challenge.

Peter's putt was fairly straight but back into the grain so pace was going to be key for his putt. It would be easy to leave it short. Peter figured there was only a four-inch break on the putt so he stroked the putt and the ball started tracking for the hole. Peter could hear the grass grabbing the ball and slowing it down, but Peter had allowed for this in his putting stroke. The ball reached the hole and grazed the bottom edge of the cup, refusing to fall in, stopping eight inches past the cup. "That's a certain par," Ben said, "take it away, Peter. Good effort."

Ben placed his ball down, removed his marker, and studied the putt. It was a short putt of four-and-a-half feet but a fast one. Ben lined up the putt and stroked the ball with only a six-inch movement of the putter on the back stroke. The ball rolled purposefully towards the hole entering right in the front door and rattling gloriously into the hole.

"Nice putt, Ben. Have you ever missed one?"

"Not unless I want to," he said, bending to pluck the ball from the hole and putting the flag back in. "Two down, Peter, but somehow I think this round could be your most rewarding ever, if you want it to be. Any money you lose will be well spent, sort of like a coaching or consulting session." Peter had to agree with what Ben said.

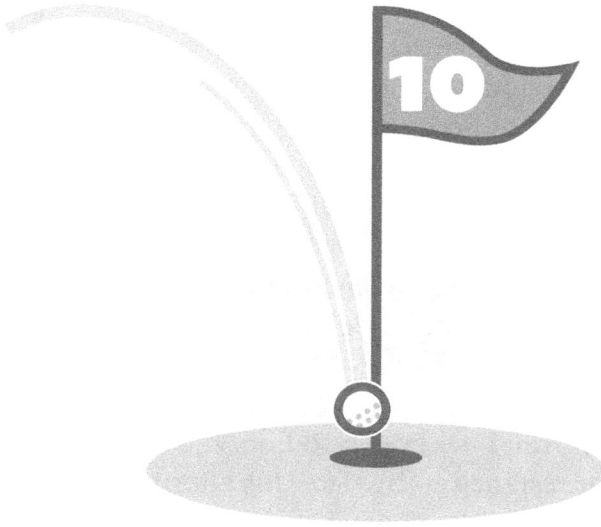

Changing Values

As they drove, Ben continued their discussion. "Most people believe I am trying to run their lives and control them. I'm not. I 'm showing them a better way but they feel they're losing too much so they resist. It's like what my son said on several occasions, 'For whoever wants to save their life will lose it, but whoever loses their life for me will find it.' People focus only on the loss, but miss the fact that there's so much more to gain—kind of like what you experienced when you saw your shot as I saw it. Pretty cool, huh?"

Peter had to admit it was, but he was thinking about the loss, Ben mentioned. *What about my job? My car? My nice clothes?*

"Don't worry about those things right now," Ben advised, and Peter made a mental note to be careful what he thought.

"It won't work," said Ben. "I'll always know."

Hole six was the shortest hole on the course, a par three of only 115 yards and a miniscule green of only 400 square feet. The designer admired the legendary hole at Troon Golf Course in Scotland called the postage stamp and admitted he had copied the said hole. The members were evenly divided as to their like or dislike of the hole, and it was known as the Wee Terror (wee being Scottish for small). Peter and Ben arrived at the tee box, which was slightly elevated and so from the tips played a good ten yards shorter than the scorecard's 115-yard description.

"My turn still, I believe," said Ben.

"Yes, I'm resigned to my fate this afternoon. Go ahead and show me how it's done," Peter said and meant it.

"Peter, I try to make it simple but people keep making it complicated. I watch people all the time; they have bad round after round not only of golf, but of life. I want so badly to help them, but they don't want it. They would rather fail with their way than succeed with mine."

Peter hated to admit it, but that made a lot of sense—and he had been guilty of it himself.

"It's the same with golf," said Ben. "We complicate a simple movement until we've created a complex one, because there's the idea that if we master the complex, or perform well, then we've earned the results."

"Take my son, for example," Ben said, looking Peter in the eye. "Look at how complicated people have made him, but who he is and what he came to do are not that complex. You don't have to work at it. Peter, do you know you have a purpose?"

"Yes, it's the goals that I set for myself," said Peter.

Ben nodded and then said, "So we're back to you steering the ship. Did you ever consider that I have a purpose for you? Would you like to know your purpose?"

"Yes," Peter said eagerly.

"Good, I would like to tell you but first let's play."

Obviously, purpose will have to wait, Peter thought.

"Yes, it will," Ben answered.

The shot facing them was truly daunting since the wind was blowing gently behind them to the green at about ten miles per hour, meaning that the green would not receive the balls kindly. They had to clear the front bunker and stop it on the tiny green, on which the grain of the grass ran from front to back. Any shot without spin saw the ball run to the back. On one side, it would end up in a bunker (five guarded this green)—not that the green really needed any more help defending its precious par three.

Let's see how God plays this one. Peter almost laughed out loud because he had that very thought many times when he played this hole. He now had a front row seat to watch it all play out.

Ben had pulled his 58-degree wedge and proceeded to tee the ball up low, just above the clipped grass. He gripped down the shaft about two inches and took one last look at the hole. Peter noticed a calmness exuding from Ben but also a focus that was rock solid. Ben's swing was fluid as usual. On impact, Peter realized just how much force Ben had created with his swing as the metal-and-ball contact sound was crisp. The ball took off on a high trajectory, seeming to gain height like a Raptor fighter plane screaming upwards at a breath-taking pace.

The ball was almost lost to Peter, such was the speed and climb of the ball's progress, which to Peter's trained eyes seemed to be heading towards the hole like a laser-guided missile. The ball ceased its heavenly climb and came down on a near 80-degree angle to its target, narrowly missing the flag. It took one short hop forward, at which point the spin Ben had put on the ball kicked in. The ball engaged reverse gear with a vengeance and tore backwards towards the hole where it hit the flag dead center and dove into the hole like a rabbit escaping an eagle attack.

Ben was still in his finish position when he turned to Peter, holding his left hand out and opened it to drop the mic. Peter laughed and said, "I don't know whether to laugh or cry. Seriously Ben, you really are too much. You're just showing off now."

"No, Peter, just having fun. Even God enjoys a bit of fun, you know. I like to prove that I still have it. Do you ever play for fun, Peter?"

The question surprised Peter and he had never thought about it, but the answer was obvious. "Never," he responded.

"I promised to talk about purpose. Peter, do you think yours is to win everything all the time?"

"Well, I, um, er," Peter stumbled for words but both he and Ben knew the answer was pretty simple. Before he could answer, however, Ben shocked him with his next statement.

"You know, we've played one another before."

"When?" Peter wanted to know.

"In Las Vegas. I was winning after nine holes when you suddenly remembered another meeting you had to go to," Ben replied.

"Oh, yeah, I was losing if I remember correctly."

"And couldn't wait to get away. I would have taught you then, but you weren't ready to hear what I had to say. I could have given you what you needed back then," Ben said wistfully.

"What do I need, Ben? Tell me what I need," Peter asked with cautious curiosity.

"What everyone else needs—a relationship with me." Ben said it in a matter-of-fact manner and then walked to the tee box. He looked back at Peter and added, "By the way, that's your purpose. To have and build a relationship with me."

Peter followed Ben to the tee box with his gap wedge, "So that's it?" asked Peter.

"Yes, I told you it's not hard" said Ben. "Sure, you have unique talents I've given you that you can use to do things that only you can do but it all leads to the same thing—building a relationship with me."

Peter had to admit he was starting to enjoy this round. Then he suddenly remembered, *Peter, you're going to be $2,000 dollars down if you don't make a hole in one!* This was a reality check. In Peter's mind, he had a compelling reason to copy the shot God or Ben or whoever he was had made. *After all, it had worked for him.*

As he set up, he was amazed at how relaxed he felt. He was so focused, he felt he could see the inside of the cup. Peter took one last look and swung. The ball took off like a bullet and Peter ended in perfect balance, already happy with the shot as it headed for the tiny but treacherous bunker-protected green. The ball descended and thumped onto the green with a ton of backspin and nearly hit the flag as it backed up and came to rest six inches in front of the hole.

"Oh Jesus," cried out Peter. "I nearly had it! That was so close. Did you see that Ben?" who was looking at Peter like a proud father.

"I did. You chose to follow me because you were in trouble. Who wants to lose $2,000, right?" Ben winked at him. "You even shouted my son's name just then. It always amuses me when I hear that."

"Hear what?" asked Peter.

"People who shout out my son's name on a golf course when things go wrong, but won't give him another thought off the course."

"Oh, sorry," Peter said blushing

As Ben and Peter moved to the next hole, they stopped at the green to pick up their balls. Ben asked Peter another interesting question: "What are you doing with your time on earth, Peter?"

Peter had no idea how to respond. Time was not something he thought much about. He had been happy working and playing golf. He and his wife had no children, so there weren't many other activities that commanded his attention. By the time they got to the next tee, he still didn't have an answer and so was relieved to hear Ben say, "Let's play this seventh hole."

"Let's," Peter agreed, "but I have to think on the time thing you asked. I guess if I had to be honest, I'm wasting a lot of time, doing the same old things for myself. I've built a great sales team and they've all done quite well financially."

Ben asked, "Did you do that for them or for you?"

Peter was stunned. He had never considered that he was using his sales team to achieve his goal of winning everything at all times.

"Do you want to know what the team says about you when you're not around? They laugh and say, 'Peter doesn't drive his BMW. His BMW drives him!'"

"Peter, there's a lot of collateral damage from what you've already done that can't be fixed. Your wife's lonely, you're living way beyond your means, and you're one economic recession away from a nervous breakdown. Carrying on as you have will only cause more damage and misery both to others and ultimately to you. I've been trying to help you since you were eleven, but you set your direction and path like the captain of your own ship."

"You were created for a purpose. Your job is to find that purpose and fulfil it through your relationship with me. When you do that, you'll find the satisfaction your toys can't give you and, believe it or not, when you help others, life will take on new meaning. Life isn't all about you!"

Since Peter was still listening, Ben continued. "I gave you life, Peter, and I have a good plan in mind for you. You know what they say when you get a new drug. You must read and follow the manufacturer's instructions. In short, I'm the potter, you're the clay. Let me mold and shape you since I know what kind of clay pot I'm making. I've done it many times."

Peter was beginning to regret they were only playing nine holes. They were on the seventh and his time with Ben was flying by. He had not felt anything like this since the summer with the Scottish pro, who had solidified his love for the game and given him much-needed advice at the time. Now, here was Ben. In this short space of time, he had taught him so much about golf but more importantly lessons about life. Little did Peter know that the best was yet to come.

PART THREE

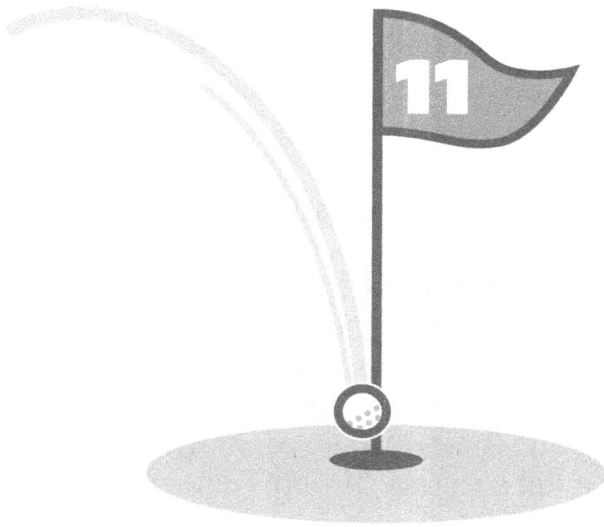

The Scottish Pro

Peter had been a good golfer since he had begun playing as a child. He was a great student in school and always studied hard, but he practiced golf even harder. After school, he would go to the course and spend at least two hours there or until it got dark. His parents had to persuade him to go outside and play catch or throw a football with his friends, or else he would have had no social time with anyone else—it was always golf. Peter's dad bought him his own set of clubs for his eleventh birthday and even though they weren't new, Peter was grateful. He had decided that being good at golf would open doors for him. Even at his young age, he knew wealthy people played golf and he wanted to be where the money was.

Peter's Dad loved golf too, but he was a frugal man, so he played at the local municipal course even though He could have afforded to go to the country club. Peter got to go to the country club twice a year when they had an open day. Peter's dad loved golf and even though he had been invited to join the country club, he stayed at the municipal course because, in his own words, "One club loved golf while the other club loved money, and I know where I would rather play."

One year when Peter and his dad played on an open day, they were warming up at the range and the club pro stopped to watch them. After ten minutes, they went to tee off and the pro followed. Peter's Dad took his first shot, then Peter. As they picked up their clubs to go to the next hole, the pro said, "Excuse me. If that's your son, he has some talent and I can see he gets it from you." Peter's Dad was unmoved by the flattery, but Peter was at full attention. The pro continued, "We have a junior program here for promising young golfers."

Peter's dad cut him off, saying "I'm not a member here."

The pro said, "I can see that," but before Peter's dad could respond, he added, "What I mean is that I know most of the regulars and their kids. I'm thinking your son's good enough to get a club scholarship."

Peter begged his dad daily to take advantage of the scholarship. His dad finally relented and Peter started attending the junior program. Despite his initial excitement, Peter eventually lost interest when he realized he was being treated differently because his dad was not a member. He dropped out after a year, went back to the municipal course, and practiced every day.

When Peter was 14 years old, a young Scottish pro came to the municipal golf club for the summer. The pro was even better than the pro at the private club where Peter had gotten a scholarship. This pro got the job after playing a round of golf with the Club Captain. Peter heard not only had the pro shot ten under par, but he helped the Captain get rid of his slice, which the Captain joked he had had longer than his wife.

The Captain claimed he played the best round of his life with the pro, so he offered him the job and had him sign a four-month summer contract 15 minutes after they finished their round. The Captain told the members, "If you catch lightning in a bucket, get the damn lid on quick or you'll lose it. I didn't want to lose this guy to any of the private clubs." The Captain never asked for references, so no one knew where the new pro was from.

Everyone soon admired the new pro, even Mr. Jones the butcher, the grumpiest man in town, who was always complaining that the club wasn't run well. The guys at the club said he was happy because the pro had cured Jones' shanking. Before the pro came, everyone made it a point never to stand by Jones' side when he played a shot. They joked that the safest place was in front or behind him.

Like everyone else, Peter respected the pro. He was in awe of his ability to shape the ball at will. Everyone, including Peter, wondered why this guy was not on tour or at least had not gone to one of the other private clubs and offered to teach. He could have made at least three times the amount he was getting and charged more money for lessons. In the four months the pro was in town, he gave more than one thousand lessons, which is more than eight lessons a day.

People were coming from 50-plus miles away to have a lesson with the Scottish pro who could sort out the most crooked, misshapen, and uncoordinated of swings. The club was suddenly thriving and after only a few weeks, the country club manager from the private club came calling, under the guise of needing a lesson. During the lesson, he offered the Scottish pro a job. All he took with him when he left was a far better swing because the pro quietly but politely refused the offer, much to everyone's pleasure and bemusement at the municipal. Why would anyone turn down such a large increase in money?

That's when the rumors started. It was said the pro was from a wealthy Scottish family and did not need the money.

Some said he was a money launderer and was leaving a life of crime. Most of the rumors were generated by those who frequented the dated club bar after a round of golf. The strange truth was that the members knew absolutely nothing about the young pro, but they all wished he would stay longer than the four months he signed for. Someone told the captain, "You were smart to sign that guy up so fast, but dumb to sign him for only four months." No one was surprised that the person who said that was the complainer, Mr. Jones the butcher.

Peter was off from school for his two-month summer holiday during the time the pro was at the club. In a bold move, Peter volunteered to shag golf balls and collect the balls between lessons at the end of each day. The pro smiled at Peter when Peter stood nervously in front of him with the proposition. "Sure, wee man. I've been waiting for someone to ask me for a summer job. Yours it is. My only question is: Can you work hard and be on time?"

"Sir," Peter replied, "if I have to run through a fire, I will be here on time."

The pro smiled and responded, "Well, let's hope it doesn't come to that, wee man."

The pro gave Peter a lesson each day as part of his payment. His dad even came for a lesson to see who his son was spending his summer with. The pro made some subtle changes to his dad's swing, which was already a fine swing, but it was the words of advice he spoke that had even more impact. Peter didn't hear exactly what was said, but caught snatches in between running around collecting balls. He heard words like, "Never stop believing, stay focused, and have faith." At the end of the lesson, they shook hands and actually hugged, something Peter had never seen his dad with anyone except him and his mom.

That night at home after dinner he said to Peter in a serious but friendly tone, "Listen carefully to everything the pro says because you could learn a lot, Son, and not just about golf."

"Yes" Dad replied Peter, slightly puzzled but glad that the pro had received Dad's seal of approval. Peter's swing was improving daily and he would have hated to see his dream summer job end early. With the lessons he was having, and all the extra information he gleaned by listening in on other people's lessons as he collected balls all day, Peter's game showed massive improvement.

He decided he was good enough to compete with the adults in competition, something that didn't go down well with the members at the club. One of the members saw Peter had come in second in the weekly medal competition and said, "I come to play golf to get away from the kids. Now I've got to play with one and get beat by him too." Peter's game kept getting better and better. Whereas before when in a bunker, he used to be happy just to get out, now he was actually trying to hole the shot. It showed how confident he had become, especially since the pro had shown him what bounce on a sand wedge was and what it was for.

Peter returned to school but was still working for the pro on weekends. He was trying to get as much information and knowledge as possible since the pro's summer contract was due to end soon. In the second week of September, Peter turned up for work. It was his last day but the range was empty. Only the young Scottish pro was there going through the clubs in his bag and seemed to be warming up. Peter walked up to the range and the pro turned and smiled, "Well, my wee man is here. How about we play the back nine, front nine is busy already?"

"Yes!" said Peter eagerly. He joined him and they both warmed up, and shortly thereafter headed to the tenth hole.

Peter had never been so nervous in all his life. He could actually hear his heart beating in his chest. The pro stood on the tee box and said, "Well, wee man, are you going to have a heart attack or play some golf? Always remember that it's just a game."

Instantly, Peter felt calm and his heartbeat slowed to its normal rate. The Scottish pro could make someone feel right at ease. Peter replied, "Yes, let's play some golf, sir."

"Good," said the pro, "and today you can use my first name. It's Sam."

What happened on that back nine over the next two hours was incredible for Peter. Sam not only gave Peter the information he'd been searching to learn but felt unable to ask, but he showed him how to do it too. At the end of the game, they went into the clubhouse to have a soda and chat. Peter had never been in the clubhouse except to receive a trophy or prize. On those occasions, he had to leave immediately afterwards because he was too young to be in the bar.

Today, it seemed Ben had gotten a pass for young Peter, and suddenly he felt quite grown up as he sat at the bar. When they finished their sodas, they went their separate ways but only after Sam had given him $100 dollars as a tip for working so hard throughout the summer. It was the most money Peter had ever held and he was overwhelmed with excitement. They shook hands at the clubhouse door, where Peter's Dad appeared to pick him up. "Invest it wisely," Sam said, "and listen to your father. He's a wise man."

Sam and his father shook hands and embraced, then the pro turned and left. A committee had formed to try and persuade the pro to stay; they were even going to offer him a wage unheard of in those days, especially at a municipal course. They never got to ask him, for even though they searched everywhere, he was gone. For weeks after the Scottish pro left, people were calling the clubhouse for lessons. Mr. Jones the butcher walked around like a dog that had lost its much-loved owner, but he never shanked again. Surprisingly he had become quite up-beat, even when playing golf. Peter always wondered what happened to that Scottish pro.

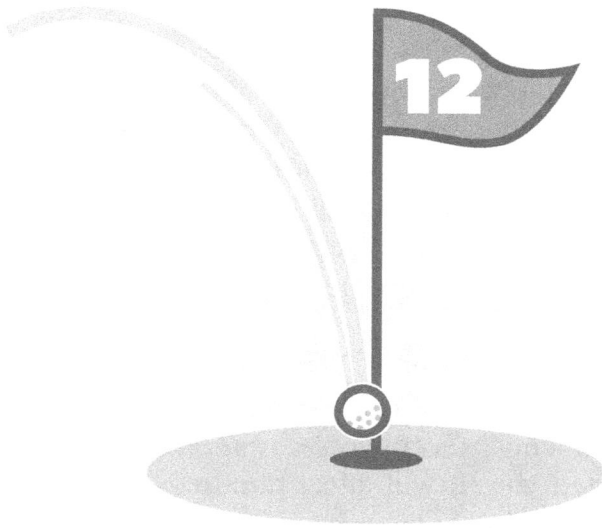

The Pro Revealed

Hole seven was a 390-yard par four with a wide fairway that ran gently downhill all the way. The hole was set up for an iron off the tee since the hole had a deep-sided stream meandering across the fairway at 265 yards off the tee. Once over the stream, the fairway started to narrow dramatically toward the green, which was guarded left and right by bunkers.

The mistake players made on this hole was thinking they could just blast away with a driver and get it close to the green. If they did that and missed the fairway, they would then have the pleasure of playing their second shot to one of the smallest greens on the course without the help of any spin—not a pleasant thing to try on this tiny green. The green was designed to reward the prudent strategist and punish the greedy.

They had driven in silence for the first 15 seconds of the trip to the next tee, until Peter without looking at Ben said,

"So this new path, Ben, what will it cost me?"

"Let's talk about the cost if you stay on the current path you're on. Let's say you go to a new company and stab your current company in the back and steal their clients when you leave your present company."

That was exactly what Peter had been thinking about doing. *So Ben really does know the secrets of my heart*, thought Peter.

Ben continued without Peter asking him to do so. "People always think there are no consequences to their actions. You will mentally scar people, your team, and your clients who trusted you. It will affect hundreds of people and when those affected people come into contact with others, they in turn will affect them with their behaviour. Peter, it's the same as when you smile at someone or do an act of kindness. The next person they meet will benefit from your actions. Wouldn't you rather have this kind of impact?"

But Ben wasn't finished. "Let's talk closer to home. Peter, your marriage won't last much longer because your wife is fed up of being treated life a trophy wife. She doesn't feel loved, so within three years, that will end."

Peter was silent but his face said it all. Ben continued, "You're right. You will get a younger version of your present wife and a bigger house, a faster and more fancy car, and you think you'll be alright. But here's the bummer of the deal. You'll still not be happy. In fact, it will just make you even more determined to go higher, earn more, and get more stuff."

Ben had Peter's undivided attention. No one had ever spoken to him so directly since he was a child. On one hand, Peter wanted to walk off the course. On the other hand, he wanted to hear more of what Ben had to say—and more was coming

"Peter, I'm sure you remember about there being a wide way and a narrow one; it's from the newer part of my Bible. It's new because the stories were written when my son came and after he rose from the dead."

Peter was amazed that Ben had chosen that story, because it was one his father's oft-used themes for a sermon.

"Yes, Ben, I know it. I heard about it all my life. Is it in Matthew?"

"Yes, Peter," Ben said. "Good to see you haven't forgotten all your training. It's in Matthew chapter seven and verses thirteen and fourteen. Since you know that truth, Peter, what path would you say you are on?"

Peter didn't want to respond, for he knew his pursuit of more prestige, more money, and more of everything was a slippery slope as his father had warned him. Still Ben waited for a response and finally Peter said, "I am on the wide path that leads to destruction."

Ben nodded his agreement and continued, "Think of it this way, Peter. One day that shiny new BMW will be a junker, all rusted out. Your job will end or someone younger, better, or more qualified will take your place. Worse, you aren't even happy with what you have. You don't enjoy your winnings because you want more. The path you are on is a dead end."

Ben let all that sink in before he added, "But it doesn't have to be that way, Peter. You can change course. It's not too late."

Peter wanted to change the subject and asked, "So where does the other path lead, you know, the narrow one?"

"I don't know," said Ben.

"What! I don't believe this! There's something you don't know?!" Peter said incredulously.

"All I can tell is that the second path leads to happiness and life, but I don't know because that path becomes what you make of it," Ben replied. "I don't script it for you, but I set the boundaries of the fairway. You follow me just like you are on this course. You watch me, follow my lead, and then make your best shot. Even if it doesn't turn out as you want, you still have the peace and joy. Peter, many follow me, but not many go all in, You know that term, right Peter?" Ben asked with a smile.

"Yes" said Peter nodding, "I do."

"Peter, what's the number one reason for a bad golf shot?"

Peter said, "Fear of failure without a doubt."

"You're right, Peter. Ben Hogan the golfer said that seventy percent of his game was mental and only thirty percent was his swing. Yet thousands of people still try to analyze the crap out of his and their swing every day."

Ben continued, "In golf, as in life, you have to give up control to gain control. It sounds crazy, but Ben Hogan said. He said if golfers would do the opposite of what they are doing now, they would play golf so much better."

"Peter, at the moment your golf's the only area where you partially give up control to get control. In life, work, marriage it's all you in control. Where would you say you have the most success, apart from the world's view of success?"

Peter looked at Ben and said "You know where, Ben, it's golf!"

"Exactly. That is the reason you keep playing this beautiful game because here on the course for that few seconds of a shot, you almost get it."

Peter sighed and said, "I know you're right, Ben, but what if you're . . . ," Peter caught himself.

"When have I ever been wrong, Peter?" Ben chuckled.

"Ok, you got me there. Never. Are you telling me that my fears are imagined and not reality?"

"No, Peter, your fears only become real when you believe they're real. It's like the guy who thinks he is going to put the ball in the water and then proceeds to put the ball in the water because he took a fear, believed it, nourished it, and let it grow, and then is surprised when he puts the ball in the water."

"Speaking of golf, my tee shot, I believe," Ben said.

"Yes, I believe it is," said Peter, realizing that the golf was the easy part of this round.

"It is, isn't it, Peter?" quipped Ben. "But that could be how your whole life is, just sayin.'"

Hole seven was deceptive. The mistake most people made was over clubbing, not realizing that the ball was landing on a downhill fairway because of the stream running across the fairway. The fairway played a little firmer because of the drainage the stream offered. Ben had chosen a four iron and gripped down about an inch and a half on the grip to take some distance off the club. Ben went through his setup, which always started with the grip and then stood over the ball, relaxed but poised like a big cat ready for explosive movement.

Peter found he loved to take in everything about Ben's swing and as he watched it unfurl, he always noticed something new. This time he noticed Ben's balance, which was impeccable and seemed to anchor his swing. He thought of the old Scottish teaching pro telling him once, "Laddie, you canna swing a golf club while out of balance since your brain is more focused on the balance problem, which is a survival skill, than on hitting a wee ball that in that moment it considers unimportant."

The pro had said that balance was important in life as well, but he had forgotten the rest of what the pro had tried to impart to him. *That old Scottish pro could play for sure, such a great swing and he had such wonderful balance, just like Ben.* Peter laughed inwardly to himself as he watched Ben's club meet the ball and send the ball away on a high trajectory, like a frozen rope, dead center of the fairway, landing at 250 yards and coming to a stop 260 yards in the center of fairway and five yards before the stream.

It was then that Ben looked at Peter and Peter stared into those eyes that had impressed him when he first saw them. The balance, the sayings, the presence, the love, it all suddenly made sense and Peter shouted out, "It was you. It was you, Ben. You were the Scottish pro. I can't believe it."

"Ay, laddie, it was I. And I'm back to teach ya again, for your old coach has never been far away," Ben said with a huge smile.

Peter thought the time with the Scottish pro had been special because he was so young. Instead, he realized the time was so pleasant because it was God's presence in his life. Then he said, "But you didn't come to teach me the Bible or Sunday School. You came to teach me golf!"

"Ay, my wee man. I knew if I could teach you golf, it would continue to teach you about life. Now I find that you are in a bit of rough, but I believe you can find your way to the fairway once again," Ben added.

Peter stood with his hands on his hips, pushed the visor back on his forehead, and shook his head back and forth. "You are just full of surprises," Peter proclaimed, and knew it was going to take him a while to piece together all that happened on what he thought was going to be a simple nine holes of golf.

"And now, please show me what you remember from what the Scottish pro taught you many years ago," Ben said, bringing Peter's attention back to the game at hand.

Peter selected his four iron and teed the ball a little higher so the ball would catch the club face a little higher up. Since he had put the ball a little forward in his stance, he also gripped down an inch so he could make a full swing, Peter placed the club behind the ball and set his body to the leading edge of the four iron and took one last look at his target (Ben's ball).

He swung, and the ball ripped straight away like Ben's ball on a gloriously high trajectory, thumping down 250 yards out and coming to a stop at 260 yards from the tee, only five yards short of the stream and three feet away from Ben's ball. Peter was slightly amazed at the feeling and the result of the shot because he had hit numerous great shots in his life but this one felt different. Then it occurred to him that it was not so much the shot but the motive or the lack of motive that had changed his mindset. He was playing golf for the joy and fun of it, not because it made him feel good to beat someone else or for monetary gain or prestige. He simply played for the pure, unadulterated fun of playing a beautiful game.

Then he remembered with a guilty conscience those weekend golf rounds with his dad years ago, which he realized were the most fun he had ever had on a golf course. Pangs of remorse pierced Peter when he thought about the pain it must have caused his dad when Peter no longer had time, or refused to make time, to play.

"You know, Peter," said Ben, knowing what Peter was thinking, "all relationships can be mended. All it takes is for both people to want it and for both people to forgive each other."

"It's easy to say, Ben, but what if someone has acted so poorly that forgiveness cannot be given?"

"Your dad loves you, Peter, and misses you greatly." Their golf balls were a near identical distance from the green but Ben was about six inches back and to the side of Peter's ball. "Me first, I think," said Ben.

Ben took out his 52-degree wedge and with a brief look at the hole, took his stance and swung a low, burning wedge with a mess of spin on it, which landed six feet past the hole. The ball spun back, just missing the hole, and ended up six inches from the hole for a gimme birdie. *Pure class*, thought Peter.

Peter was relaxed but excited. He pulled out his 52-degree wedge and looked at the shot. It was ten yards downhill, but there seemed to be a slight breeze coming straight back at them, which would eliminate the downhill gain and bring the distance back up to the 130 yards to the front edge the pin. *It was a full shot perfect,* thought Peter. He settled the grip onto the club and set the club over the ball, focusing on the shot. He could see it a full wedge on a low trajectory with a little draw and a ton of spin because of the trapped contact the club was going to impart to the ball.

Yes, thought Peter, *I can see it.* He started the swing and confidence coursed through him into the club. It seemed they were one, his mind body and club working perfectly in unison. The contact felt pure and as Peter's head moved up into the finish position, he saw the ball heading toward the green, maxing out at forty feet in height, then curving with the draw towards the pin like metal to a magnet. The ball landed six inches past the pin, spinning in its own divot as if it was trying to bury itself, climbing out of the divot eventually and coming to rest one foot in front of the pin.

As they started the short drive to the green to pick up their golf balls, Peter had thoughts emerge he had not considered in years. *How much more do I have to go through today? Has this Ben or God come to torment me?*

"If you don't say it, I can't help you with it," Ben offered, urging Peter to face his feelings.

"I don't want to," Peter said, "and what good would it do anyway?"

"Your anger will eat you up if you don't," Ben countered. "In fact, it already is."

"I don't get it, Ben, I don't get it," Peter finally revealed. "You can make a golf shot look so easy, but you could not save my mother. She believed in you. She prayed and so did my father. Hell, I even prayed for my mother to get well but she didn't. She died right in front of me, drugged on morphine, and I heard her last words: 'It's beautiful.'"

By now, Peter had tears running down his face. "Where were you, Ben, where were you? Were you playing golf that day?" Peter surprised himself by what he said, but Ben stayed calm. Peter was not prepared to go this deep, especially on the golf course where he had worked all his life to control his emotions. He looked around and was still amazed and relieved that there was no one else around, just him and Ben.

"Peter, your mother was only yours temporarily," Ben responded. "It is written that whoever lives in me will never die. She is in another place."

Peter interrupted, "Heaven?"

"Yes, she is in heaven where she is very much alive as we speak. As you see it, death is final, but not to me. Your mother transferred to another realm, and you and your father will one day as well."

Ben let those words sink in before he continued. "When your mother said, 'It's beautiful,' she was referring to all the family being together, in a place where there are no arguments, tensions, or worries, where people live like you've experienced at times today, in a natural state of being with me. Your mom and all those others who know me and have gone on before live there. Would you want to deprive your mother of that opportunity?"

"No, but it hurts and still hurts," Peter said, tears still flowing freely. There were tears of sadness but also tears of hope, a hope that Peter had not considered or wanted to accept. There was consolation that his mother was actually alive and one day they would be reunited, if Peter would choose differently.

Ben reached over and hugged Peter, whispering, "It's okay, Son, it's okay."

Peter looked at Ben. "My mother would be so disappointed in me today. She warned me life wasn't all about things. There was a day when I believed in you, in Pappa, as mom used to call you. Did I let you down too?"

Ben held Peter's head in both hands and looked directly into his eyes. "You were lost, Peter, but now you're not. I'm not concerned about let downs because I expect them. I am just so happy to get my wee little fella, my Petey, back."

"I've not been called that since mom died," said Peter.

"Shall we go and pick up those balls and play the next hole? Oh, by the way, you stopped the bleeding but that's still $3,000 I am up to now."

"Thank, God,"

Ben interrupted, "You're welcome!"

"Thank God, I mean Ben, that we are only playing nine holes," Peter said with a smile.

They drove in silence the short distance to the green, but the mood was quite different than when they had first met. Both golfers were smiling, although Peter was still wiping away tears. He wanted to ask more questions about his mom, what it was like, did she think of them, but Peter realized he had time on his side. Ben was not going anywhere any time soon.

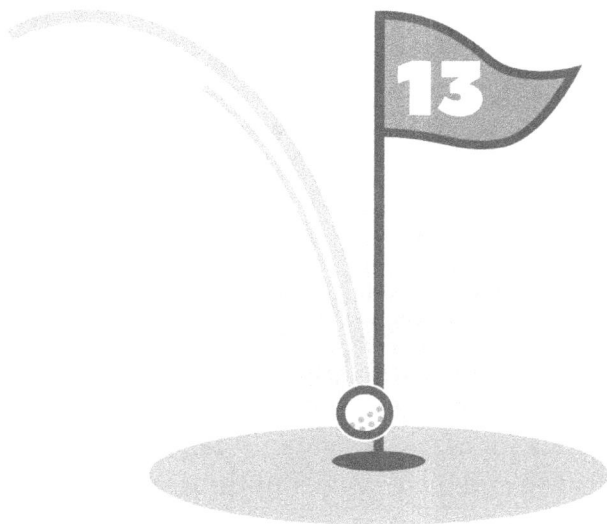

The Prayer

Hole number eight is a long par five demanding either strategy or simply long hitting. To attempt to reach the green in two shots takes on all the trouble that the designer purposefully put into the design of this hole. Off the tee, the fairway turned left at 290 yards and the corner of the fairway was protected by a large bunker and a swale of deep grass.

If golfers cleared the bunker, they were then faced with an as-the-crow-flies carry of around 300 yards, depending on how far they cleared the bunker from the fairway that turned again left 100 yards from the bunker to the green, which had a marsh in the front. It was pointless to take on the tee shot unless the golfer intended to go for the green in two shots.

To do so, players needed to be committed and a long hitter if they used a more strategic approach and had a great short iron game—then a one-putt birdie was a possibility. If they played it as three shots to the green, at worst they took a par five and were happy. What usually happened was that players on this hole get caught in between a mindset of part strategy and part attack, which never went well and usually resulted in a bogey or worse. As the saying goes, a double-minded man is weak in all his ways.

As they got out of their golf cart, Ben turned to Peter and asked, "Shall we start over?"

"You mean the bet?" Peter asked.

"No, I mean our relationship," said Ben smiling.

Peter thought for a moment and then said, "I would like that. We have a lot of catching up to do." Peter knew both his mom and dad would be pleased, but this time he was starting over with Ben for himself.

"Yes we do," said Ben, "and where better to get to know someone than a golf course. One of the things I love about golf is that you reveal your true self on the course. Four hours of golf is too long to hide. It all comes out: love, hate, anger, bitterness, or needs. That's why I have a special place in my heart for golfers. You're a brave group prepared to play a game and be seen by all when you're emotionally naked. If you want to employ someone, you only need to play a round of golf with them and you would know their morals, values, and level of integrity without any scientific profiles."

"I get what you're saying," said Peter, "but you said their needs would show on the course?"

"Yes. All people have a need and that need will sometimes overpower common sense, even their morals and values. Take this hole, for example. The designer really knew what he was doing. What person arriving at this hole doesn't want to drive over the corner with a powerful drive and impress his friends? Right there the golfer has been forced down the wrong path—the broad path leads to destruction and narrow is the path that leads, in this case, to par." Ben was on a roll, but Peter interrupted.

"So you're going for it in two after that sermon?" asked Peter with a smile.

"Heck yes, said Ben. "If you can, you should. If you can't, you shouldn't. I can so I will. The trick is to let your real self-make the decision and not your ego." After the ball was teed up, Ben surveyed the shot and then moved into the ball.

Looking at him, Peter felt the lack of any negative emotion or motives like Ben had mentioned such as pride, ego, or bitterness, Ben looked perfectly relaxed and poised. It always amazed Peter that golfers were so obsessed about hitting the ball but seldom got the fundamentals of a swing right.

In Ben's grip, stance, posture, and balance Peter saw perfection and thought it must be almost impossible to hit the ball badly from such a solid and strong foundation. Ben started the driver back neither hurried nor rushed but almost slowly. The club reached the zenith of its backswing and was pulled down by the combination of perfect timing and balance until the club head smacked into the back of the ball, sending it screaming into the blue sky.

It was at impact that he could truly understand the power that was being delivered in an effortless way. He remembered an old teaching pro telling him that a golfer creates force in a swing but can't use force to get force. What he had seen unfold was a perfect display of this principle. The ball was just right of the bunker but with a tad of draw that was working the ball in the right direction around the slight dog leg. The ball cleared the bunker while on the descent but still 30 feet in the air, hitting the fairway like a scalded cat and scampering on to finish 350 yards off the tee and to the left of the fairway, in perfect position to go for the green in two,

"Great shot, Ben," Peter said, "but why do I keep saying that? You can't do anything else! I can see that you have committed to going for the green in two."

"Yes, I quite like this hole," Ben responded.

"I get the feeling you had some input into the design of this course," Peter said half jokingly.

"Ha, that's right, Peter. The designer did pray for guidance and I did help him as I help anyone who asks. The great thing is that he listened for my reply."

Peter nodded and asked, "How am I going to follow that drive, Ben?"

"Once again, you don't have to beat what I did. You only have to copy it. Don't beat me. Work with me."

Peter looked at the hole and in his mind he could see what he wanted for his shot—the flight of the ball as well as the ball drawing over the bunker to hit the fairway and run out to the left-hand side of the fairway. Peter took his stance and felt the tension release from his mind and body. Peter knew that a good swing was not the absence of tension, it was the correct use of it in the swing. He took one last look at the fairway and settled. He then made a small trigger move that initiated his swing—a slight bump of the hands towards the target.

Peter's swing started in his feet and worked up his body almost in slow motion to the observer, but it created an enormous amount of leverage. The club started down slowly for the first eight inches of the downswing but quickly became a blur as it approached the ball, making contact with that noise that an observer who is a golfer instantly knows as a perfect contact. It is a sound that cannot be described but once heard, it is forever remembered.

Peter finished in perfect balance and watched the ball on its trajectory as if he was controlling the ball with the thought he had before he started his swing. The ball cleared the fairway bunker, with a touch of draw, scampering on after landing and coming to a stop so close to Ben's ball that a beach towel thrown down would have covered them both.

Ben said nothing but gave Peter a high five.

"I've hit longer on this hole but I've never hit it better. It was so easy. For so long, I played every shot to beat my opponent, to hit it closer or further. That's the first time I hit a shot to copy someone."

"Welcome back, Peter, you're getting free and not fighting yourself." They started the drive down the cart path to the fairway, and Ben said, "Peter, explain more to me about it being easy."

"For too long, I've been just marching to my own beat. To be honest, I didn't realize how tired I was. My plan to get richer and more powerful just isn't working. I have moments of joy but they're short and hard-earned."

Then he did something he had not done in a while. He gave his dad some credit. "After losing my mother and his wife, my dad still has a joy that radiates from him even though he has so little compared to me. It annoyed me but today I think I understand it."

"Your dad isn't as poor as you think. True, he has an older pickup truck and lives in the same house you hated. But he has no debt and also has three other houses he has rented out. His investments have done well and I've blessed him. In truth, he's a multi-millionaire."

Peter's mouth flew open in shock. He was speechless.

"Truth is, Peter, your father has followed me his entire life. He sought me, prayed, and listened. He didn't try to beat me or do things his own way, and it has worked. What's more, he's happy and has joy. You chose a different path and you're unfulfilled and unhappy. So who has made the better choice?"

"If you're not for me, you're against me. I know that sounds harsh. There's a battle going on and you need to pick a side. Take your time but you do need to choose sooner rather than later. Time for our second shots. I think it's me first?"

Peter was deep in thought while watching Ben play his shot. If he was to go for the green 250 yards away, he would have to carry the ball all the way since the marsh welcomed little white golf balls like a greedy miser. Once they entered, they never left until the annual dredge of the marsh to recover the 3,000-plus golf balls that ended up there annually.

Ben selected his five wood, a club Peter did not carry since he thought the club a little old school but carried a hybrid club in place of the five wood. After eye balling the shot, Ben stepped up, settled over the ball, and with one last look, swung. The ball sped away laser-like to its target all speed and spin as the 19 degrees of the five wood made it soar upward while at the same time it went forward. It seemed to Peter to be doing both very well.

Peter knew instinctively when the ball had cleared the marsh and it was just before this that the ball had started its descent to the distant green. The ball landed eight feet past the pin and stopped virtually in its own pitch mark.

"Well, it's getting a bit boring but great shot, Ben," laughed Peter. "You want me to follow that?"

"Considering the ball is on the green and I'm putting for eagle, I would say yes, you should imitate my shot," Ben answered.

"I surrender, I surrender," said Peter. "There's one problem with playing your shot. My hybrid is not enough club and my three wood is too much. If I grip down on the three wood, I get the distance but the wrong trajectory."

"Very true, Peter, which is why you need this," said Ben, holding out his five wood,

"You're going to loan me your five wood so I can follow your shot? Why would you do that, Ben?" said Peter, with a surprised look on his face.

"Why would I say 'follow me' and then not help you to follow me? I'm not trying to trick you or make it impossible."

Peter took the five wood out of Ben's hand and walked to his ball. The lie was perfect and he had the right club. It was as a tour caddie would say, a stock five wood, meaning a normal full swing, nothing more or less was required. The shot was not the problem. Peter knew what to do and how to play it. It was the other question that was eating him up.

If he said yes and followed God, he knew that everything would change—that his life would not be the same. Was he ready for that? Did he want that? He remembered what Ben had said: "Why would I ask you to follow me and not help you?"

Peter turned to Ben and said, "Okay, I want in, I'm picking my side. I want to follow you, so I guess I'm *all* in."

Ben smiled and gave Peter a thumbs up.

Peter turned back to the ball and set up to hit the shot. His shoulders felt relaxed, like he had cast off a huge weight. The shot Peter played was a mirror image of Ben's, coming to rest nine feet behind the pin and one foot from Ben's.

"You did it, Peter. You can show me the line," Ben laughed.

"I will do my best to help," Peter said, handing the five wood back to Ben, then added, "I need to pray, Ben, don't I?"

"Sure do, Peter, and let's start with the most basic one. I think you all call it the sinner's prayer. 'Dear Lord, I know I am a sinner and I ask for your forgiveness. I believe your son died on the cross for my sins and I invite you into my life and heart. I want to trust and follow you as my Lord and Savior. Amen." Peter shut his eyes and repeated the prayer.

"Welcome home, Son," said Ben. "Now let's finish this hole."

The drive to the green was quiet for only a short while, until Peter said, "It's all going to change for me, isn't it, Ben?"

Ben turned to Peter and said, "I hope so or today would be a waste of time for me. you, and your dad. You can either embrace change or fight it, but change is like the tide coming in. It's going to happen, so it's up to you to fight or embrace it."

They had arrived at the green, and both pulled out their

putters. They both marked their balls and then Peter surveyed his putt as Ben stood to one side. From his crouched position behind the ball, Peter looked over at Ben and said, "Hey, I thought I was following you on this hole. So why am I putting first?"

"First, because you are farthest away and second, like any good father, I want you to go from following me to me walking alongside me. In a small way, I am allowing you to lead this time for if I've trained you properly, you'll know the right path. Right now, it's a nine-foot putt for eagle. In the future, it will be much more important things. Once I'm gone, my spirit abides in you to help you know what to do. I'll give you my mind."

"Wow," said Peter, "so no pressure then?"

"None at all, Peter. In this case, the worst that can happen is you'll lose another $1,000 dollars."

Peter laughed and said, "It just gets better and better," and went back to picking the line of the putt. Looking at it, Peter could not make his mind up between three or five inches of break on this slippery downhill putt, so for the first time he thought, "What would Ben do?" As he looked, he saw the line of the putt unfurling before his eyes, like it had always been there but a mist of tension and fear of missing the putt had created a confusion that had been hiding it. It was three inches to the left from the outside of the cup.

Peter put his ball down and removed the marker. He then moved in and set the putter behind the ball, took one last look at the line and the hole, took a deep breath, and stroked the ball. Peter watched the ball track down the imaginary line and enter smack bang in the center of the hole, rattling around in the cup till it came to a stop. "Yes!" shouted Peter. "Eagle!"

Ben wasted no time but went through his usual setup routine, placed the putter behind the ball, and stroked it on the identical line to match Peter's eagle and half the hole.

Peter was enjoying himself and was actually looking forward to the ninth hole, even though he was $3,000 down with no chance to catch up. He had indeed paid for his lessons, but they were priceless and would pay dividends for all eternity.

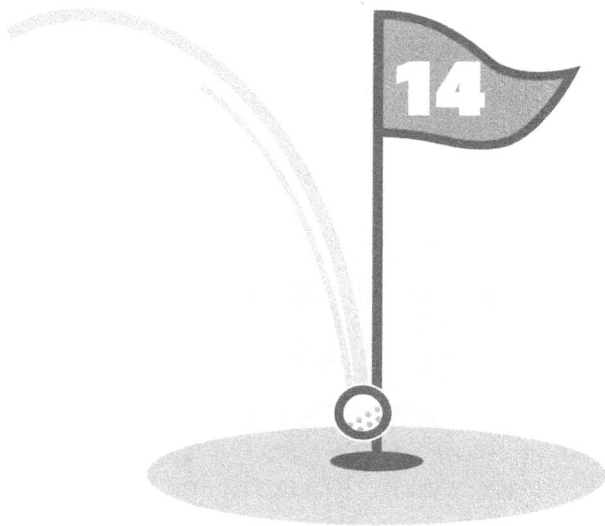

Learning a New Game

Hole nine was a longish par four of 430 yards from the tips. The only problems with this hole was that it played straight back into the wind, thus adding length to the hole. There was out of bounds both left and right, and 250 yards off the tee there was a bunker on the left side of the fairway and at 280 yards a bunker on the right. These bunkers were there to intimidate because they could be carried by the bigger hitters, though the fairway itself was nearly 40 yards wide—the most generous thing the designer had done on this hole.

On many golf courses, it is the perception of possible trouble that makes the players tighten up and then compound one bad shot after another, and in many cases on hole nine, players were happy to record a double bogey six with a sense of relief. "My, what a nice hole," said Ben looking at the pristine fairway and view that unfurled before his eyes.

"You act likes it's the first time you've seen it, which I

doubt," said Peter, half joking.

"It's the first time I've played it, although I've seen it many times. The view never gets old."

Peter said, "You're going to have to help me out a bit, since I'm a new member of this club, so to speak."

"No problem, Peter," said Ben.

Ben was looking down the line, "By the time some golfers get here, they are frustrated and annoyed. They feel that they need to finish strong on the last hole of the front nine to somehow vindicate themselves and show their playing partners they can still play this game. In effect, the designer got into their head but not even in the way he intended."

"Explain, please," Peter interjected with a smile, "in language I can understand."

"He didn't build the course to break people; he built the course to build the people. I must admit, Peter, that I got a little tired of you playing the course well but learning nothing. Instead of learning from the course, you tried to master and dominate the course so you wouldn't have to change."

"So you watched me play? So why did you choose to come today?"

"I'm always watching, Peter, never too far away, and the reason I'm here is simple—I'm answering your father's prayers."

"My dad?" Peter exclaimed, and then said more softly, "My dad."

"Yes, when we played a round when I was the Scottish pro, I promised your dad that I would look out for you, and he regularly reminds me of the promise. It's nice that he does, but there's no need. I never break a promise."

"Without his prayers, you could've given up on me?" Peter asked.

"I don't usually give up on anyone, even after repeated rejections. It's sometimes in the smallest of acts that I see hope. For example, you've never cheated at golf, have you, even though you could have gotten away with it on numerous occasions?"

Peter replied, "Never! I know what that feels like, I would rather die than cheat at golf. Just to think about it is . . . " Peter paused and then finished his thought, "is distasteful in every way."

"That's true, but you don't take the same philosophy into your business life, do you?"

"Well, there are times in business . . ." Peter began, but before he could finish, Ben started lining up his next shot. Ben chose his three wood and surveyed the shot. There seemed to be no wind but above at the tree tops on both sides of the fairway. Ben could see a bit of movement, indicating maybe a five-miles-per-hour breeze.

Peter wasn't paying attention at this point. He was reeling from Ben's latest revelation and insight into Peter's work life, the things he kept private. Ben swung and the contact noise was to Peter what Beethoven is to a classical music buff. The ball flew away on a slightly lower-than-normal trajectory that Peter knew would not be affected by the slight wind because it kept below the canopy of the tree-lined fairway. The ball came down and struck the center of the fairway midway between the two bunkers at 265 yards, running on until it stopped dead center of the fairway at 290 yards—140 yards from the front edge of the green. The pin was right in the middle of the green, leaving a shot to the fluttering flag on the green of 152 yards in total. *A nice eight iron from there*, thought Peter

Peter acknowledged Ben's tee shot with a smile and a thumbs up, and also took his three wood and moved to the tee box. All Peter had to do was follow Ben's shot—no more and no less. Peter doubled down on his focus and his pre-shot routine. The split second before his swing started, he felt poised and powerful, but even more, he felt mentally sharp and at peace. Peter started his swing and the contact of club and ball was perfect. The ball flew on a low trajectory just like Ben's, hitting the same position between the two bunkers, scampering on to rest within six feet of Ben's ball.

Ben whistled through his teeth and they took what was to be their last ride in the cart. Peter turned to Ben and asked, "So what happens next Ben? This is the last hole, so where do I go from here? How am I supposed to function after this meeting?"

Ben patted Peter on the forearm, "All in good time, Peter. Let's finish what we started first and then you can buy me a good glass of wine in the bar and we'll discuss your path for the future. Seriously, don't worry about the future, Peter. It's of no use worrying. You can change the present and that will change your future. And you can follow me."

Peter wanted to ask more but they had arrived at their balls. As they stood there, the shot to the green revealed itself. The pin was in the easiest pin position they had enjoyed all day. The greenskeeper knew the mind of the golfer, for when the pin is in the middle, most players relax since all they have to do is put the ball on the green. This false sense of security causes some to settle for a "good enough" shot, so they relax and often don't focus on exactly what they want to do.

"What do you see, Peter?"

"I see an eight-iron hit on a slightly lower trajectory straight at the flag, because it will stay below the tree tops. I'm going straight at the flag. If I waver in my shot commitment, I'll either be left or right of the flag, which is still good. How do you see it, Ben?"

"About the same, except I'd not play it to be anything but a straight-at-the hole shot. That's what I want you to do with your life. Don't think you were a pretty good person who didn't cheat at golf. I am not looking for people who settle for 'good enough.' I require people to aim for the ideals and commands I established."

"Uh, I was just thinking of making par on this hole, and you are making it a life lesson about following you?" Peter said shaking his head.

"Well, you asked," Ben said, "play the best shot and go for the pin—all in."

Peter nodded his head, feeling pretty good that he saw the shot just about like Ben did. Peter looked at his target and everything started to fade away—the bunkers on either side of the green and the breeze above the tree tops. Also, he felt his need to impress his father and to win at all cost melt away too. Left was just the pure joy to get out of his own way and play the shot.

Peter had hit thousands of golf balls in his life, but he had never experienced such a combination of feelings in one shot. The ball never deviated from its intended purpose, landing three feet past the flag and backing up with a little spin to rest four inches from the hole for an inevitable tap-in birdie three on the par four.

Peter stood back to watch Ben one more time. It was more of the same: perfect swing, the ball screaming toward its target, landing twenty-five feet past the hole, only to have the backspin carry it back to within three inches of the cup. Peter knew he was a better golfer and hoped he was a better man after only nine holes of being with Ben.

As they drove to the last hole, Peter was quiet, waiting for the rest of what Ben had to say. They tapped in their putts and Peter said, "Follow me to the bar. Drinks are on me," then realized Ben undoubtedly knew the way on his own.

Ben said, "Sounds good. I need to sign my card and collect my winnings!"

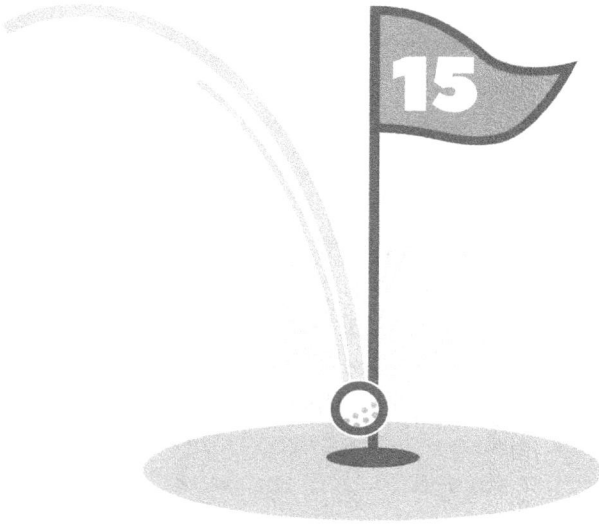

The 19th Hole

Peter sat on the terrace outside the clubhouse and saw Ben shaking Brad's hand, giving him his clubs back. They talked for quite a while and Ben patted Brad on the shoulder. Then Ben turned to join Peter at the bar. There were two glasses of red wine waiting. Ben sat down and picked up a glass and held it out. "Peter, to new beginnings and to this beautiful game," then clinked glasses and took a drink. There was silence for a while, then Ben spoke. "So what's next, Peter?"

Peter grinned, "What, no chit chat? Just straight into it?"

Ben didn't respond, but kept his gaze fixed on Peter.

"Well, I haven't had a chance to think it all through, but it starts with going home and talking to my wife."

"Good start," Ben chimed in.

"We need to look at where we live, maybe downsizing and moving closer to dad, who isn't getting any younger. I need to work on our relationship."

"That's all good, Peter, but why not talk to your father about this?"

Peter turned to see his dad walking across the club-house lounge and bar towards him. Both Peter and Ben rose to greet Peter's father and then both gave him a warm hug.

"Wow, Dad this is a surprise. What are you doing here? I mean, I'm glad you're here, but it's quite a drive for you."

Robert said, "I got a call last night from Ben and he asked me to drive up to meet with you and him. I needed a day off and I had just finished restoring an old Shelby Mustang that needed a test run so it was a perfect opportunity."

Peter's father turned to Ben and said, "I travelled 260 miles because of your call. I wouldn't ordinarily do that because of a call from a stranger, but I felt like I know you. It's strange but the way you spoke was so familiar, like how in my quiet time I relate to . . ."

Then suddenly Robert clasped his hand over his mouth and whispered, "My God!"

"Yes indeed, Robert, I am he."

Robert moved forward and hugged Ben again with tears coming down his face. "Thank you."

"It's no problem, Robert. It's what I do and I'm happy to be here." Ben motioned to the bar to bring an extra glass of wine. "Shall we sit? We have lots to talk about."

There was silence for a few seconds and then Peter spoke. "Dad, I'm sorry for my behavior, for the way I have treated you, and for the things I've said. I'm going to talk to Julie about quitting my job and selling the house. There are going to be changes for sure."

"Good," said Robert. "In fact, I have a house that you can live in rent free if you like. It's a great house with nearly 2,000 square feet of space in a great area. It's yours if you want it."

"Wow, are you serious? After the way I've treated you."

Robert smiled and replied, "I've never been more serious. I'm your father just like Ben. We love you despite some of the things you've done and said. We both forgive you, so the offer is there. Take your time and think about it."

"Thanks, Dad, and thank you, Ben. That was a heck of a nine holes of golf. Pity we did not keep a score card. Somehow I don't think I'll ever play so well and lose like that again.

Ben reached into his pocket and slid a half-completed scorecard across the table. "Keep this so we can play the back nine soon. It will remind you not of the scores but of the words spoken and the paths chosen, of relationships healed and most importantly of all that took place because of a father's love. Peter looked at the card and was amazed to see the numbers in front of his eyes.

		Ben	Peter
Hole 1	par 4	3	3
Hole 2	par 4	2	2
Hole 3	par 3	2	3
Hole 4	par 5	3	3
Hole 5	par 4	3	4
Hole 6	par 3	1	2
Hole 7	par 4	3	3
Hole 8	par 5	3	3
Hole 9	par 4	3	3
Par 36		23	26

"That's a card I'm going to keep for a long time," said Peter.

'Remember the nine holes we played, but more importantly, what we talked about. The round isn't finished until the 18th hole, so you'll see me soon so we can finish this round, and I can see how you're progressing now that you're on the right path," Ben explained.

Peter reached for his checkbook and said, "There's the small matter of the $3,000 I owe you."

"Tell you what, Peter," said Ben, "put it toward your

moving expenses."

"Well, I must get off," Ben said. All the men stood and hugged one more time.

Ben looked at Peter and said, "I never have and I never will give up on you."

Robert added, "Neither will I, Son."

Ben added, "You must remember that if you need help, ask and then listen. I'm not a shouter, so be attentive."

Robert said, "Thanks again, Ben," and with that, Ben turned and walked off.

"Well, Dad, there's a lot to do and it's not going to be easy."

"It's true," said Robert. "It's always easier to do the wrong thing than the right, but tell me what are you doing this Saturday? Maybe we can talk it over during a round of golf?"

"Sounds good," said Peter, eager to apply what he had just learned during the most amazing nine holes of golf in his life.

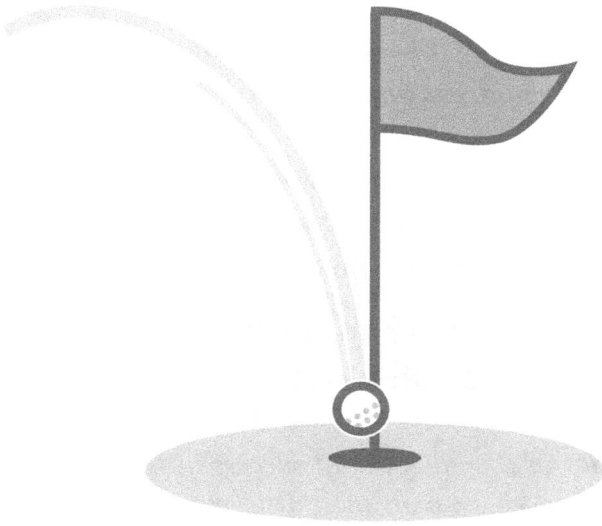

An Interview
With the Author

Andrew Linch was interviewed about his novel, *Drive for Show, Putt for Dough* to explain more about the story and the lessons found in the book.

* * * * * * * * * *

Q: Let's talk about your book. There is a part where Peter as a teenager goes to a party with his friends. He is basically enamored with the big house and it seems to have quite an impact on him. Can you tell us a bit about that?

Andrew: Well, actually that is from my own life. I was in primary school and about eight when I was invited to a boy's party on a new estate. I went to this house and it was on a lovely plot of land. His name was also Andrew and his parents had the nice car and everything in the house was new. It brought into focus for me how my house wasn't like this. I decided then I wanted better and more than my parents had.

Q: *How did that impact how you related to and viewed your father?*

Andrew: I saw him as someone who was not achieving, not a winner in life. This was based on the fact that I didn't know the other parents, if they had a good marriage or bad marriage or if they were up to their eyes in debt. Obviously, I had eight-year-old eyes, and I decided that was what I wanted, which was happiness and success as I thought I saw them.

Q: *You talk a lot in the book about success in terms of material things. Can you share with us a little more about why that theme was so prominent?*

Andrew: By the age of twenty-one, I was earning more than my father. I looked in the paper one day in London and realized I could actually buy a Ferrari, which I wanted to do very badly. Buying it was not the problem, but insuring it was, because the bill would have been astronomical for a twenty-one-year old. It was not the love of cars that was driving me to own a Ferrari. It was the fact that people would see me driving it and think, *There is Andrew Linch. He is very successful.* That was my motive, not simply owning a lot of fine Italian cars.

Q: *Do you think that's a drive for most men, wanting to be seen as successful?*

Andrew: Without a doubt, it is. The reason men are out polishing their cars on a Sunday is so that anyone who sees them on Monday sees a nice shiny car. No one wants to turn up in a dirty, never-clean car. What's the point of working hard at a job you don't like, making payments on a car you can barely afford, just for it to be all muddy and dirty? So, yes, the wash and polish are very important for what they represent and what people will think.

Q: *So presumably, you no longer see your success backed up by material things?*

Andrew: No, I don't, and it has taken me a long time to get there. After mixing and working with many very wealthy people, I realized they are no happier when they are wealthy than the person who is poor. Yes, they can pay their bills, but that's about the only thing they have over the poor person. I remember meeting a high-net-worth financial adviser who had been doing the job for fifteen years. He told me he had never actually met a happy multi-millionaire. I said it couldn't be true, that there must be *someone* who was a multi-millionaire and was happy. He said, truthfully, there wasn't and reiterated that he had never met a happy multi-millionaire.

Q: *So how do you now define success?*

Andrew: If it isn't by material things, then you have to think about what you were made or created for. Let's go back to the Ferrari. People often ask what one does in a Ferrari and I would say they go very fast because that car was created to go very fast. There is nothing worse than seeing a Ferrari go along at 30 miles per hour, because that's not what it was made for. The same is true for people, whether we were made to go fast or slow or high or low, we have to find what God created us to do and step into that. Everything else is truly just stuff or possessions. No amount of stuff or possessions or a house with five bedrooms and bathrooms is going to make us happy. It's just like plaster that is covering up the problem; the problem is we were not made to be happy with stuff. We were made to be happy through purpose and serving God and other people.

I tried to present in *Drive for Show* that our stuff is just that: it's for show. The second half of the saying is *Putt for Dough,* and that's where the most important activity is in life. Peter had to come to grips, with Ben's help, that the "drive" part of his life was flawed, and that he would be held accountable for the "dough" part, which was how he treated people and related to God. I hope the reader will come to grips, like I did, with the fact that there is more to life than golf, possessions, or winning. Life is about relationships and values, and the most important values are God, family, and integrity.

To contact Andrew Linch, please go to his website
www.andrewlinch.com